Whitehall Paper 78

T0299960

Less is Better
Nuclear Restraint at Low Numbers

Malcolm Chalmers

www.rusi.org

Royal United Services Institute for Defence and Security Studies

Less is Better: Nuclear Restraint at Low Numbers
By Malcolm Chalmers
First published 2012

Whitehall Papers series

Series Editor: Professor Malcolm Chalmers
Editors: Adrian Johnson and Ashlee Godwin

RUSI is a Registered Charity (No. 210639)
ISBN 978-0-415-81422-5

Published on behalf of the Royal United Services Institute for Defence
and Security Studies
by
Routledge Journals, an imprint of Taylor & Francis, 4 Park Square,
Milton Park, Abingdon OX14 4RN

SUBSCRIPTIONS
Please send subscription orders to:

USA/Canada: Taylor & Francis Inc., Journals Department, 325 Chestnut Street,
8th Floor, Philadelphia, PA 19106, USA

UK/Rest of World: Routledge Journals, T&F Customer Services, T&F Informa UK Ltd,
Sheepen Place, Colchester, Essex CO3 3LP, UK

All rights reserved. No part of this publication may be reprinted or reproduced or
utilised in any form or by any electronic, mechanical, or other means, now known or
hereafter invented, including photocopying and recording, or in any information
storage or retrieval system, without permission in writing from the publisher.

Contents

About the Author

Professor Malcolm Chalmers is director of research at the Royal United Services Institute, London, and leads its work on nuclear policy issues. He is a special adviser to the UK Parliament's Joint Committee on the National Security Strategy, and has been a visiting professor of defence and foreign policy in the Department of War Studies, King's College, London, and a special adviser to Foreign Secretaries Jack Straw MP and Margaret Beckett MP. Professor Chalmers has also been professor of international politics at the University of Bradford; visiting fellow at the Center for International Security and Arms Control, Stanford University; and senior consulting fellow, International Institute for Strategic Studies.

His recent publications include: 'Kingdom's End?', *RUSI Journal* (Vol. 157, No. 3, June/July 2012); 'Looking Beyond the Chicago Summit: Nuclear Weapons in Europe and the Future of NATO' (a joint Carnegie/ Brookings/RUSI paper, written with George Perkovich, Steven Pifer, Paul Schulte and Jaclyn Tandler, April 2012); 'Arms Control after START', in Nichols, Stuart and McCausland (eds.), *Tactical Nuclear Weapons and NATO* (Carlisle, PA: US Army War College, April 2012); 'The End of an "Auld Sang": Defence in an Independent Scotland', RUSI Briefing Paper, April 2012; 'Forging UK-China Consensus on a Strengthened NPT Regime', RUSI Occasional Paper, March 2012; 'Small Nuclear Forces: Five Perspectives', RUSI Whitehall Report, 3–11, December 2011; 'Words That Matter? NATO Declaratory Policy and the DDPR', in Andreasen and Williams (eds.), 'Reducing Nuclear Risks in Europe', NTI, 2011; 'Nuclear Weapons and the Prevention of Major War' in Bruno Tertrais (co-ordinator), *Thinking About Strategy: A Tribute to Michael Quinlan* (Paris: Fondation pour la Recherche Stratégique, 2011); 'Looking into the Black Hole: Is the UK Defence Budget Crisis Really Over?', RUSI Briefing Paper, October 2011; 'Comparing UK and Chinese Nuclear Force Development', *Peace and Development* (Beijing) (June 2011); 'If the Bombs Go: European Perspectives on NATO's Nuclear Debate', RUSI Whitehall Report, 1–11, May 2011; 'Continuous At-Sea Deterrence: Costs and Alternatives', RUSI Briefing Note, July 2010; 'Nuclear Narratives: Reflections on Declaratory Policy', RUSI Whitehall Report, 1–10, May 2010; 'NATO's Tactical Nuclear Dilemma', RUSI Occasional Paper, March 2010 (with Simon Lunn); and 'Britain's New Nuclear Debate', *RUSI Journal* (Vol. 154, No. 2, April 2009).

Acknowledgements

As I have developed this paper, I have been fortunate to have been able to present some of the ideas that it contains at seminars and conferences around the world, and to listen to perspectives from experts hailing from all of the world's nuclear-armed states. Paul Schulte has been a frequent companion at many of these events, and I learnt much from our frequent discussions and jointly written projects, as well as from his persuasive comments on this paper in draft form. Shashank Joshi, my RUSI colleague, took time away from writing his own monograph on Iran's nuclear programme to provide detailed feedback. I owe a particular and heartfelt debt to James Acton for his thoughtful, detailed and incisive comments on an earlier draft. James has already written several excellent papers on deterrence at low numbers, all of which provided inspiration for this work.

I would particularly like to thank Ashlee Godwin and Adrian Johnson for their tireless editorial efforts. The paper would have been much poorer without their insistence on clarity and conciseness.

This paper was made possible as a result of the financial support of the Nuclear Threat Initiative in Washington, DC, which has consistently supported RUSI's nuclear work for several years.

Acronyms and Abbreviations

ABM	Anti-ballistic missile
BMD	Ballistic missile defence
CBW	Chemical and biological weapons
CTBT	Comprehensive Test Ban Treaty
DDPR	Deterrence and Defence Posture Review
DRDO	Defence and Research Development Organisation (India)
EPAA	European Phased Adaptive Approach
FMCT	Fissile Material Cut-Off Treaty
GDP	Gross domestic product
ICBM	Intercontinental ballistic missile
INF	Intermediate-range nuclear forces
MIRV	Multiple independently targetable re-entry vehicle
MTCR	Missile Technology Control Regime
NAS	National Academy of Sciences (US)
NATO	North Atlantic Treaty Organization
NPT	Nuclear Non-Proliferation Treaty
NSNW	Non-strategic nuclear weapons
OECD	Organisation for Economic Co-operation and Development
SALT	Strategic Arms Limitation Talks
SLBM	Submarine-launched ballistic missile
SSBN	Ballistic missile submarine
SSOD	Special Session on Disarmament
START	Strategic Arms Reduction Treaty
UK	United Kingdom
UN	United Nations
US	United States of America

I. INTRODUCTION

The number of nuclear weapons in the world's arsenals has been reduced by around 80 per cent over the last two decades. Yet, as the US's 2010 Nuclear Posture Review made clear: 'both [the US and Russia] still retain many more nuclear weapons than they need for deterrence.'[1]

The purpose of this paper is to examine how, and under what conditions, further cuts in these stockpiles could be made. It argues that steep reductions are possible if all seven established nuclear-armed states accept as an objective 'nuclear restraint at low numbers', defined as a situation in which each country feels comfortable with a stockpile numbering less than 500. If this objective were accepted, it would make possible a further 80 per cent reduction in the global military stockpile: from 11,500 warheads in 2012 to around 2,000 in the early 2020s. The main responsibility for achieving this objective would fall on Russia and the US, which still possess more than 90 per cent of the world's nuclear stockpile; but the five other states (China, France, the UK, India and Pakistan) would also have to take steps to restrain the size and capabilities of their own forces, and to show that they are doing so.

The Benefits of Restraint

Further restraint and reduction in the arsenals of the world's five recognised Nuclear-Weapon States would contribute to fulfilling their disarmament obligations under the Nuclear Non-Proliferation Treaty (NPT), and strengthen their hand in arguing for continuing restraint from the treaty's Non-Nuclear-Weapon States. The NPT's 'grand bargain' between its nuclear and non-nuclear members may not be the main reason for the nuclear abstinence of the latter. If the Nuclear-Weapon States were now to argue that no further reductions were possible, however, it could do significant damage to the legitimacy of the treaty at a time when it is already under strain as a result of the nuclear programmes of North Korea and Iran.

---

[1] US Department of Defense, 'Nuclear Posture Review Report 2010', April 2010, p. ix.

Table 1: Estimated Military Stockpiles of Nuclear Warheads, 2012.

Russia	5,500
US	5,000
France	300
China	240
UK	225
Pakistan	90–110
India	80 100
Israel	80
North Korea	<10
TOTAL	**11,500**

Source: Federation of American Scientists, 'Status of World Nuclear Forces 2012', *fas.org*, accessed 15 August 2012. These totals exclude several thousand warheads, mainly in the US and Russia, that have been removed from military stockpiles and are awaiting dismantlement.

Yet even if the NPT did not exist, the major powers would need to take seriously, and consider what measures can be taken to reduce, the risks that existing nuclear arsenals pose to international security. Some nuclear weapons, during some time periods, are more dangerous than others. The risks that they pose, moreover, vary depending on the domestic and international political context in which they are held. However, in every country, risks could be reduced – or increased – by changes in nuclear doctrine (planning on how weapons might be used) and capabilities (what is available to be used).

The wider political benefits of nuclear restraint are also important. Nuclear weapons remain one of the most important indicators of whether, and how far, the major powers are able to manage their relationships in a co-operative manner. If states are vigorously building new, and more capable, strategic systems against each other, this can contribute to wider tension between them. Successful restraint amongst existing nuclear-armed states, on the other hand, can engender trust, as well as providing mechanisms for reducing the risks of rapid escalation in the event of limited conflict.

Some might criticise the scenario for nuclear restraint as overly ambitious. Others might feel that, by focusing on requirements for 'minimum deterrence' rather than on complete nuclear disarmament, it is not radical enough. At the very least, however, it is hoped that the reader will see it as providing some food for thought as to how the international community should respond to what remains a real, and potentially catastrophic, risk.

Outside the Tent

The main focus of the paper is on the seven states whose possession of nuclear weapons is, in practice, not under serious dispute, and which have openly declared that they possess these weapons. However, two further states possess nuclear weapons as of 2012, and more could follow over the next decade. Any discussion of how to move to nuclear restraint at low numbers has to take some account of these states.

Of the non-established nuclear-armed states, Israel is widely believed to have the greatest capability, both in terms of quality and quantity. It is believed to have an arsenal comparable in size to India's and Pakistan's (around 100 warheads), as well as a range of delivery systems. Yet it has never openly declared its capability, a policy of opacity which still contributes to regional stability. Israel's participation in multi-actor nuclear restraint could be of increasing importance, especially if others reduce their arsenals sharply. In the short term, prospects for such restraint depend more on relations with, and restraint by, potential nuclear-armed states in its neighbourhood, notably Iran and Saudi Arabia. If regional nuclearisation were to draw the established nuclear-armed states into more explicit nuclear alliances with states in the region, however, Israel's strategic relationships with extra-regional powers (such as Pakistan) would become more difficult to ignore.

Possible developments in the capabilities of other states, such as Iran and North Korea, also need to be considered. Even if the size and sophistication of their nuclear forces develop slowly at first, their nuclearisation is spurring further investment in missile defence (especially by the US), with all the difficulties this poses for relations between the larger nuclear powers. The acquisition of nuclear weapons by previously non-nuclear NPT states could also undermine the credibility of the treaty's 'grand bargain', weakening the case for deeper reductions by the recognised nuclear states.

The impact of Iranian and North Korean nuclearisation on prospects for nuclear restraint between the existing powers would depend on whether the two countries continued to be treated as nuclear 'outlaws', or whether (as in the case of India) a *modus vivendi* were reached in which their new status was reluctantly accepted. This latter scenario would become much more likely, in the case of Iran, were Saudi Arabia to acquire its own nuclear arsenal. Were this to ultimately lead to both countries being accepted as *de facto* nuclear-armed states, the risks of nuclear conflict could increase, and the negotiation of new confidence-building measures would become more relevant than ever. However, the content of such measures could be significantly different from those that are appropriate to a world with only seven acknowledged nuclear-armed states.

Although it already has a rudimentary nuclear-weapon capability, the prospects for eventual legitimisation of North Korea as a nuclear-armed state are even fewer than they are for Iran. Due to the close alliances that Japan and South Korea have with the US, and the domestic stability of their regimes, the risks of onward proliferation are not as strong as in the Middle East. There is also an expectation that regime change in Pyongyang could one day allow a reversal of its nuclear programme. Such a reversal would be in the common interest of the US and China – and indeed of Japan – and could serve as an incentive for co-operation in a future North Korean crisis.

Focused Restraint and Appropriate Transparency

Achieving an 80 per cent reduction in existing stockpiles over the next decade will require, most of all, steep cuts by Russia and the US. At this stage, however, the negotiation of a completely new US-Russia Treaty would distract from progress towards this objective. The existing New START (Strategic Arms Reduction Treaty) agreement already provides a good framework for counting and verifying their deployed strategic warheads and missiles, which continue to have the greatest destabilising potential. The possible use of such systems in a disarming first strike continues to be an important driver for the maintenance of large arsenals by both countries, and concerns over these capabilities could be a source of increased tension in times of intense international crisis. It makes sense, therefore, to focus the next steps in reduction and restraint efforts on these systems, including a mutual, incremental reduction in New START-counted deployed warheads from the current treaty's ceiling of 1,550 warheads each to around 700–800 by the end of the decade.

In parallel with this reduction in strategic systems, the US and Russia could aim for co-ordinated reductions in non-strategic nuclear systems, but focused – as in the case of New START itself – on operationally deployed weapons rather than on the warheads themselves. This could be attractive to both Russia and the US.

Russia is reluctant to reveal information about its non-strategic nuclear capabilities, seemingly content to create the impression of large numerical superiority in this field. Yet, because of its reliance on dual-capable delivery systems (aircraft, ships and defence missiles) for operational deployment of NSNW (non-strategic nuclear weapons), the size of its deployed non-strategic arsenal has probably fallen sharply in the last two decades, in line with the size of its conventional forces. One recent study suggests that it might have as few as 1,000 non-strategic weapons deployed with operational units.[2] With further rationalisation of Russia's conventional force structure likely to take place, this number could fall further in coming years.

The US is also under political pressure to make further reductions of its own, with NATO's latest Deterrence and Defence Posture Review

---

[2] Igor Sutyagin, 'Russian Non-Strategic Nuclear Potential: Developing a New Estimate', RUSI Occasional Paper (forthcoming, 2012).

committing the Alliance to exploring ways of doing so as part of a reciprocal process with Russia. As a result, the US may be able to meet its requirement for NSNW in Europe with an arsenal that is significantly smaller than the 180 or so warheads currently deployed there. Therefore, provided that the prospect of a new, 'all-encompassing' arms-control treaty does not persuade the two sides to preserve current arsenals as 'bargaining chips', the next decade could see significant reductions in deployed NSNW arsenals on both sides.

The US remains far ahead of Russia in its plans for deployment of missile defence capabilities; and the possibility of a further step-change in the US's capabilities in this field is one of the central reasons which Russia has given for continuing high levels of investment in its own strategic nuclear missile forces. Yet current US ballistic missile defence (BMD) capabilities for use against Russian long-range missiles remain very limited, and planned NATO deployments will not change this materially. Russia could also hedge against the possibility of a US missile defence breakthrough by retaining the ability to rapidly rebuild its deployed offensive forces.

If the US and Russia do reduce their deployed strategic arsenals below 1,000 warheads each, there will be increasing pressure on the other nuclear-armed states to show that they are also restraining their arsenals. A possible early step could be for all seven states to join a New START-modelled information exchange process. In addition to the long-range missiles in their arsenals, the smaller nuclear-armed states could also be asked to declare, and verify, their deployments of medium-range, ground-based missiles (forbidden to the US and Russia under the Intermediate-Range Nuclear Forces [INF] Treaty), as well as holdings of medium-range aircraft and sea-launched missiles.

If the process of mutual nuclear restraint is to evolve from a bilateral to a multiplayer exercise, it will probably have to rely more on mutual restraint and transparency, rather than the treaty-based numerical limitations that have been at the heart of US-Russian arms control since the 1970s. This would probably still involve most, if not all, of the five other nuclear-armed states maintaining arsenals lower than those of the US and Russia. The UK has already announced a reduction in its arsenal to fewer than 200, and India and Pakistan might not build up to the UK's level, on current trends, until around 2020. Provided that all seven states committed to the goal of restraint at low numbers, however, it would be unnecessary and indeed counterproductive to seek to enshrine this in a treaty-based formula. Nor would it be reasonable to expect the smaller nuclear-armed states to agree to permanent 'no increase' commitments, at least as long as the US and Russia still possessed much larger forces of their own, and their missile defence capabilities also remained unconstrained.

The focus of efforts to seek nuclear restraint at low numbers should be on encouraging restraint and transparency in relation to deployed warheads on long-range missiles. Further transparency in relation to other, second-echelon capabilities – such as warheads in storage and fissile material production capabilities – should be encouraged. However, restraint in relation to these capabilities could be less stringent, allowing states the option of maintaining a hedge against future developments that could threaten their minimum retaliatory capabilities. Allowing states to retain possibilities for future build-up could help to persuade states that it is safe to make deeper reductions in the forces that they need to deploy now.

The Risk of Losing Control

Chapter II explores the most important argument in favour of further nuclear restraint: the possibility that nuclear weapons could actually be used. Faced with an international crisis, and under levels of stress and uncertainty for which they may be poorly prepared, individuals and bureaucracies could take steps that lead to nuclear use becoming a real possibility. Indeed, this possibility is fundamental to the value of these weapons as a deterrent. For, in seeking to demonstrate the credibility of 'deterrent' threats in times of crisis, nuclear-armed states would be under considerable pressure to prove that they were as prepared as their opponent to carry them out if provoked.

Nuclear weapons have never been detonated, except in tests, since 1945. The average annual probability of their use remains relatively low; but a return to the levels of risk faced in the early 1960s – when President John F Kennedy estimated the risk of nuclear war as 'somewhere between one in three and even' – cannot be ruled out.[3]

It is not hard to imagine scenarios for a nuclear crisis during the next decade. Israel, the US and Saudi Arabia could find themselves in a confrontation with Iran as it crosses the nuclear threshold. India could mobilise its army in response to a Pakistan-originated terrorist attack, prompting Islamabad to disperse its nuclear weapons. The US could find itself in a deepening confrontation with China in the western Pacific, or with Russia in its near abroad.

---

[3] Graham Allison, 'At 50, the Cuban Missile Crisis as a Guide', *New York Times*, 15 June 2012.

Why Low Numbers Matter

The consequences of even a limited nuclear war would be many times greater than any natural disaster or accident of the post-1945 period. The risk of even a handful of weapons exploding should help to deter states from a serious conflict with nuclear-armed states whenever nuclear use is a possibility. Yet the additional deterrent value of more nuclear weapons declines thereafter: the possibility that fifty nuclear weapons could explode on UK cities is not ten times the deterrent of the possibility of five exploding. Both are to be avoided at (almost) any cost.

Yet, even if the deterrent value of nuclear threats is not proportionate to their destructive potential (beyond a certain threshold), the human consequences of nuclear war would be likely to increase proportionately until much larger numbers of nuclear weapons were involved. As the number of detonations rose, moreover, the risks of wider effects on the earth's climate, and on global food production, would also increase. Even a 'limited' India-Pakistan nuclear war, it has been estimated, could lead to a substantial reduction in global mean temperatures for several years.

Some might argue that seeking to reduce the damage that a nuclear war would cause could increase its probability. However, there is little evidence to support the proposition that, for example, Russia or India would be more willing to risk nuclear war if only 10 million of their population were at risk rather than 100 million.[4] Above a certain level of assured destruction, therefore, the additional deterrent value of added destructive capability is probably negligible. A move to nuclear restraint at low numbers, therefore, could help to reduce the damage that would be likely to result from nuclear war, if it took place, without significantly increasing the danger that deterrence would be weakened.

Such considerations, nevertheless, do set lower limits on what 'low numbers' would mean. If a nuclear-armed state believed that its nuclear-armed opponent only had a fractional chance of getting one nuclear weapon onto its territory in a retaliatory strike, it might (in some circumstances) gamble that a surprise attack could limit the risk to its own society to acceptable (if still undesirable) levels. It is not easy to estimate the level of destructive capability that would be needed to avoid this risk, based as it would have to be on perceptions of the political calculus of leaders and regimes in situations of extreme stress. However, a capability to assure the destruction of ten to twenty separate targets with

---

[4] James Acton makes a similar point in James M Acton, *Deterrence During Disarmament: Deep Nuclear Reductions and International Security*, Adelphi Paper 417 (Abingdon: Routledge for IISS, 2011), pp. 27–30.

nuclear weapons is widely considered to be enough to provide a very considerable deterrent. Depending on the allowances that are made for missile and system failures, missile defence interception and other factors, maintaining an ability to destroy this many targets might require an arsenal of, perhaps, 100–200 deployed warheads.[5]

The Logic of Restraint

Another key element that supports the logic of restraint is the diminishing role of nuclear weapons in security policy. Their non-use in military action since 1945 has made it easier to persuade Non-Nuclear-Weapon States to refrain from acquisition: the expense and trouble involved have simply not been worth the hypothetical gains. The existence of the NPT, together with US extended deterrence arrangements, have further added to the political costs that could result from attempts at acquisition. Non-use has also made it difficult for those states that do have nuclear weapons to define the circumstances in which they could proportionately, and thus credibly, threaten to use them. The use of nuclear weapons, in a pre-emptive strike, in order to deter their use by others remains the most credible deterrent threat. Threats to use nuclear weapons to respond to threats to the very survival of a state could also appear credible. Beyond these two basic scenarios, however, nuclear threats may seem so disproportionate as not, in practice, to be credible.

This does mean that there is a nuclear 'taboo': preparation for the use of nuclear weapons is still socially acceptable in all of the nuclear-armed states, and in the US's main European and Asian allies. Yet, as NATO's Strategic Concept recently reaffirmed, the circumstances in which the Alliance would have to contemplate the use of nuclear weapons are now 'extremely remote'.

Other nuclear-armed states vary in the extent to which they rely on nuclear weapons. China and India have declared their commitment to use nuclear weapons only in retaliation to their use by others. Pakistan and Russia, by contrast, both maintain the option to use nuclear weapons first, primarily in response to invasion. Some of the most difficult challenges in seeking nuclear restraint at low numbers, as a result, relate to these two states.

---

[5] For a calculation along these lines by a former deputy director of Pakistan's Strategic Plans Division, see Naeem Salik, *The Genesis of South Asian Nuclear Deterrence: Pakistan's Perspective* (Oxford: Oxford University Press, 2009), pp. 304–06.

National Cultures and Nuclear Restraint

Fear of a large-scale war between the major powers remains remote. Furthermore, the appetite for the use of nuclear weapons in more limited conflicts is now much less than some declaratory policies might still be taken to imply.

The more remote and less specific the threat of nuclear war becomes, however, the more states will tend to view nuclear policy through the lenses of domestic politics and national strategic culture. Debates on weapon systems and numbers take on a highly symbolic character, often out of all proportion to their operational or deterrent value. Debates on nuclear policy become more about political relationships within countries, rather than between them.

The shared Cold War experience of Russia and the US as superpowers make it difficult for them to move more quickly towards nuclear restraint at low numbers. The two countries, over many decades, invested a large proportion of their monetary and intellectual wealth in building the capabilities that they possess today. Leading national companies, and the hundreds of thousands of workers they support, continue to depend on the maintenance of large and sophisticated nuclear arsenals. These economic drivers, in turn, reinforce national conservatism in security policy, making it more difficult for political elites to divert resources from maintaining nuclear forces.

Yet support for further nuclear reductions in the US, in particular, continues to be strong. Almost every post-war US president has embraced the ultimate goal of nuclear abolition, while the large margin of conventional war-fighting superiority, developed since 1990, has deepened interest in making further reductions in the role that nuclear weapons play in national doctrines. There is still significant resistance to formal acceptance of mutual nuclear vulnerability with Russia and (even more so) China. Some analysts still argue that the risks of building first-strike capabilities as a means of enhancing deterrence are less than those of accepting vulnerability to nuclear attack in a possible future crisis. These concerns are reinforced by the difficulties that, these critics argue, would be involved in demonstrating the credibility of nuclear guarantees to Asian and European allies if, in doing so, the US itself could be put at risk. In practice, however, the US's key non-nuclear allies (Germany and Japan in particular) have been amongst the strongest supporters of further nuclear reductions.

Moving towards mutual nuclear restraint at low numbers could make US acceptance of its nuclear vulnerability more politically salient. Whether arsenals are small or large, however, it is hard to imagine that the US could ever build such strong disarming counterforce capabilities that it could guarantee its invulnerability against other major powers (such as Russia and China) that are determined to counter such efforts. The wide range of voices in the US nuclear debate make it difficult to predict what the next steps in its policy are likely to be. It would be surprising if the next decade does not see significant further reductions in the nuclear stockpile. The pace and shape of these reductions will depend, most of all, on the contingencies of national politics. While the numerical balance between the US and Russia may have little operational significance, at least at current numbers, it retains significant political importance in Washington. It is hard to imagine that the US would be prepared to cut the size of its deployed strategic arsenal significantly below that of Russia.

If operational necessity were the primary driver of its nuclear policy, Russia could be persuaded to make further mutual cuts. It already fields fewer strategic warheads than the US (1,492 compared with 1,737), and also has fewer nuclear-armed submarines, long-range missiles and heavy bombers. Whether or not the US follows suit, the footprint of Russia's deployed nuclear forces seems set to decline further over the next decade.

Russia's current leadership, however, may be reluctant to agree a new treaty without US concessions on its missile defence programmes, and it may prefer to proceed with a more informal process of mutual reductions that would allow it to retain more reconstitution options than a new treaty would probably allow. The US could provide useful political cover by making clear that it would match any Russian reductions in its deployed strategic forces with reductions of its own.

Such a process of mutual restraint may, however, be complicated by Russia's desire to maintain a clear margin of numerical superiority in relation to third powers. Its leaders still view its possession of one of the world's two large nuclear arsenals as one of the few remaining areas of national strength. Its sphere of influence has shrunk to a fraction of what it was in the 1980s. Widespread concern, dating back to the 1970s, that the US could use its technological edge in conventional military capabilities to threaten Russia's strategic forces – through BMD and conventional strike – further feeds the elite's sense of being encircled by a powerful and expansionist opponent.

The assertive declaratory policy of Russia's political and military leaders, in these circumstances, plays both a domestic and an international role. Russian leaders do not believe that nuclear weapons are a panacea for the multiplicity of security threats that they face, especially internally. However, they do fear that other major powers may seek to exploit its many weaknesses, either through sponsoring regime opponents or (in the case of China) attempting to gain political control of outlying territories. From this perspective, Russia's nuclear arsenal can still play an important role in deterring interference in its affairs by other major powers; and, in the longer term, can allow it to maintain a hedge against the possible re-emergence of more serious threats to its territorial integrity, either from NATO or China.

If the US and Russia were to contemplate the possibility of mutual reductions to below 1,000 deployed strategic warheads apiece, both would want reassurance that China continue to exercise restraint in its own nuclear force. Most independent estimates currently suggest that China possesses fewer than 300 warheads in its arsenal, of which perhaps only fifty would be defined as 'deployed strategic warheads'. However, China has not confirmed these estimates, and a few experts have suggested that its total arsenal could be closer to 1,000.[6]

China has so far been able to use US-Russian numerical preponderance, together with the greater importance of opacity for a small nuclear force, as plausible rationales for remaining on the periphery of international discussions. If US and Russian reductions were to increase pressure on China to be more transparently restrained, however, it would be likely to trigger a vigorous internal debate. Joining the other nuclear-armed states in restraint could appeal to those who are genuinely committed to China's declaratory policies of No First Use and minimum deterrence. Some elements in China's security elite could argue that US and Russian reductions would present an opportunity to use its greater economic resources to build a more sophisticated nuclear capability, reinforcing efforts to build conventional military advantages over its neighbours. But others would argue that China's nuclear posture should continue to be based around a credible second-strike capability. This goal could require the deployment of larger and better protected forces, possibly alongside submarine-based and multiple-warhead missiles. It could also mean maintaining the ability to build larger forces in response to future developments in US capabilities. Given its wider economic and (increasingly) military strengths, however, China shares US interest in reducing the salience of nuclear weapons in international security. China's agreement to further transparency and restraint, even if Russia and the US were to undertake further reductions, could not be taken for granted. But it would be a necessary condition for moving towards a broader nuclear restraint at low numbers. And it would not be in China's interests to be seen as the main obstacle to such a process.

---

[6] Henry D Sokolski, 'China's Nuclear Weapons and Fissile Material Holdings: Uncertainties and Concerns', testimony before the US Economic and Security Review Commission investigating 'Developments in China's Cyber and Nuclear Capabilities', 26 March 2012. For a detailed Russian analysis of China's posture, see Alexei Arbatov, Vladimir Dvorkin and Sergey Oznobishchev (eds.), 'Russia and the Dilemmas of Nuclear Disarmament', Institute for World Economy and International Relations (IMEMO), 2012, especially pp. 31–35. Arbatov et al. argue that 'Beijing's reluctance to engage in nuclear arms limitations may be ... meant to obscure the huge surplus of China's nuclear capability rather than its "small size" and "weakness"'.

Further US and Russian reductions would also trigger debates in the two European Nuclear-Weapon States. The UK, with the smallest arsenal of these, would strongly welcome progress towards wider nuclear disarmament and, having announced a unilateral reduction in its total nuclear force to 180, of which only 120 will be deployed, might consider a reduction to an even lower level if the US and Russia were set on much steeper reductions. France continues to be NATO's leading disarmament sceptic, and its leaders would probably seek some reassurance that mutual nuclear restraint was not simply a way-station on the road to nuclear abolition. However, in the context of its own growing fiscal problems, France might also be prepared to make some contribution of its own, perhaps making further reductions in its warhead stockpile.

Most of India's leaders would also welcome further US and Russian reductions, which would be consistent with its longstanding commitments to nuclear abolition. It would be harder, however, to persuade it to accept restraint in relation to its own arsenal. Providing that China and Pakistan were also adopting a measure of restraint, however, India might not want to be the last obstacle to achieving mutual restraint in Asia. Much would depend on timing. As of 2012, India is still in the early stages of the development of a nuclear triad. Within a decade, India would be looking at whether it needed to go further in building up its force. Were it to do so, in the face of prospective reductions by other major powers, it would make it harder for the others – and China in particular – to continue to exercise unilateral restraint. A particularly important indicator of possible Indian overreach would be if it continued to develop, and then deployed, intercontinental missiles capable of reaching the US. An Indian decision to proceed with such a development, inconsistent with a declaratory policy focused on Pakistan and China, could significantly complicate efforts at wider mutual restraint.

Pakistan could be the hardest nut to crack for projects of nuclear restraint, given its geopolitical weakness and its consequent heavy reliance on nuclear deterrence. Yet these very factors may also make it more ready to agree to some restraint in return for greater recognition of its own concerns. Pakistan has, by a large margin, the smallest defence budget of all the nuclear-armed states, and one that is also heavily reliant on external financial support. High levels of investment in fissile material production over the next decade, moreover, mean that it should be able to build a nuclear arsenal of around 200 warheads by the early 2020s, comfortably in excess of the levels that some of its own experts have estimated are needed for 'minimum deterrence'. Like other conventionally vulnerable states, it would want to preserve some hedge capability, for example against developments in Indian missile defences. It would also need to reassure the international community that it had given up any plans for possible transfers of nuclear technologies to other states (such as Saudi Arabia or North Korea). However, it could also benefit from the international acceptance of its nuclear weapons programme that would be a necessary trade-off in return for its commitment to transparency and restraint measures; and it could also legitimately request that it get Nuclear Supplier Group exemption status similar to that which India obtained in 2008. If Pakistan were to reject such a deal, it could risk drifting into an international nuclear 'outlaw' status similar to that now facing Iran, but without oil. Given such a choice, and with its position as a nuclear-armed state now acknowledged and accepted, Pakistan might also be willing to join a wider regime of nuclear restraint.

It is also possible, unfortunately, to imagine a scenario in which efforts to achieve mutual restraint fail, and in which the three Asian nuclear-armed states embark on a surge in their capabilities that would make global nuclear restraint at low numbers unachievable. If such a surge in capabilities were to occur, however, it would have symbolic and political consequences well beyond military-technical discussion of nuclear balances. It would symbolise a return to an age of great-power confrontation, and with it an increased risk of major war. Such an expectation, even if overly pessimistic, would in turn have considerable political and economic costs.

Given these wider consequences, it still seems more likely that the major powers, however hesitantly, will not want to give up on the possibility of further mutual nuclear restraint at low numbers.

II. CATASTROPHIC RISKS

> Thus far the chief purpose of our military establishment has been to win wars. From now on its chief purpose must be to avert them. It can have almost no other useful purpose.[1]

Ever since their use against Japan at the end of the Second World War, the destructive power of nuclear weapons has been a stark reminder of the unprecedented calamity that a further all-out war between major powers would involve. However, the widespread desire to avoid such a conflict has not been accompanied by a similar degree of consensus on how best to do so.

There is no agreement as to whether the existence of nuclear weapons was a necessary, or indeed sufficient, condition for the prevention of major war over the last six decades.[2] The nature of the post-war political order – in which, over time and under US leadership, democracy became the predominant form of political organisation, prosperity grew rapidly as a result of economic globalisation, and most of Asia and Africa emerged from colonial rule – may have been (and probably was) much more important. War may also have been prevented, in part, because of the stabilising effects of Cold War bipolarity, in which the US and the Soviet Union progressively delineated clear spheres of influence. As the crises over Berlin and Cuba in 1961 and 1962 attest, however, this delineation was by no means easy to achieve or maintain. Even those who confidently assert the war-preventing role of nuclear deterrence in the Cold War, moreover, are often less convinced that the acquisition of nuclear weapons by further states (such as North Korea, Iran and Saudi Arabia) would have a similarly pacifying effect.[3]

---

[1] Bernard Brodie (ed.), *The Absolute Weapon: Atomic Power and World Order* (New York: Harcourt and Brace, 1946), p. 76.

[2] For further discussion, see Malcolm Chalmers, 'Nuclear Weapons and the Prevention of Major War' in Bruno Tertrais (co-ordinator), *Thinking About Strategy: A Tribute to Michael Quinlan* (Paris: L'Harmattan, 2011).

[3] See, for example, the widespread criticism of Waltz's argument that an Iranian bomb would contribute to war prevention. Kenneth Waltz, 'Why Iran Should Get the Bomb: Nuclear Balancing Would Mean Stability', *Foreign Affairs* (July/August 2012).

While this paper draws on the key intellectual traditions in this field, therefore, it also emphasises the importance of studying specific states, and the relationships between them, in approaching current policy dilemmas. Nor should the role of contingency – or chance – be underestimated. It is both humbling and frightening to remind ourselves that the greatest nuclear challenges of the coming decades may not yet figure at all in current discussions. A credible approach to nuclear policy, therefore, needs to be both measured and adaptable.

Approaches to Nuclear Weapons and War

Deterrence Works
For those who can be described as 'deterrence optimists', the non-use of nuclear weapons in military strikes over the last sixty-seven years is confirmation that nuclear deterrence works. The world's major powers are more cautious and risk-averse, they argue, because the potential use of nuclear weapons makes it abundantly clear what the impact of major war would be: an immediate, and inescapable, level of destruction that would dwarf even the horrors inflicted on their peoples in the Second World War. Even during the intensely ideological confrontation of the Cold War, both sides avoided using nuclear weapons against each other; in the decades that followed, they argue, the pacifying impact of nuclear deterrence has been felt even more strongly.

The benefits of nuclear deterrence, for this school of thought, have been amplified by the 'extended deterrence' that the US has provided to NATO and Asian allies, allowing them to benefit from the war-preventing quality of nuclear weapons without themselves having to invest in national nuclear forces. Only nine countries out of a total UN membership of 193 possess nuclear weapons;[4] but many other countries – such as Japan, South Korea, Australia, Canada, Germany, Italy and Japan – have security policies based on a US 'nuclear umbrella'. Nuclear weapons, therefore, are much more ubiquitous in international security policy than the relatively small size of the 'club' of nuclear-armed states might suggest.

The Betterment of Human Nature
'War optimists', by contrast, argue that the slow pace of nuclear proliferation since the 1960s reflects the fact that nuclear weapons have made very little difference to the course of post-1945 history. Thus John Mueller argues that 'the possession of such expensive armaments actually conveys in almost all cases rather little advantage to the possessor. In the

---

[4] This includes North Korea, which tested nuclear devices in 2006 and 2009.

main, they are difficult to obtain, militarily useless, and a spectacular waste of money and scientific talent.'[5]

It is understandable that Western leaders in the 1950s, emerging from the horrors of two world wars in the space of three decades only to find themselves in a highly militarised confrontation with the Soviet Union, viewed nuclear deterrence as the last best hope for avoiding another war. Indeed, threats to use nuclear weapons, together with mobilisation of nuclear forces, did play a key role in superpower confrontations during this period. Perhaps unsurprisingly, this period also saw the start of national nuclear weapons programmes in the UK, France, China, Israel and India. Of today's nine nuclear-armed states, all but two (Pakistan and North Korea) had some significant nuclear weapon capability by 1974 (the year of India's 'peaceful nuclear explosion'). In subsequent decades, however, the pace of successful proliferation has slowed. New aspirants have taken longer to develop a full capability, and more of them have given up – or been forced to give up – their efforts to do so.[6]

Since the end of the Cold War, moreover, the argument that nuclear weapons have been the primary factor in preventing inter-state war has been replaced by a more complex set of explanations. This reflects, in part, awareness amongst existing nuclear states that an overly optimistic espousal of the benefits of nuclear deterrence might be seen as encouraging the acquisition of nuclear capabilities by others, including potential adversaries; but it also reflects the growing impact of 'war optimism' on our understanding of the causes of peace and war.

No analyst of international affairs can fail to be struck by the remarkable solidity of the peace between the states of Western Europe that emerged after 1945, and which continued to deepen even as the threat from the Soviet Union vanished at the end of the Cold War. Not only has the period of peace between the great powers now lasted for longer than at any time in historical memory; the incidence of war between smaller states and, since the early 1990s, the number of civil wars and their severity, has also fallen sharply.[7]

One of the most important factors in this trend was the strengthening of the norm against changing borders by force. Attempts to build national

[5] John E Mueller, *Atomic Obsession: Nuclear Alarmism from Hiroshima to Al-Qaeda* (New York: Oxford University Press, 2010), pp. xii–xiii.
[6] Jacques E C Hymans, 'Botching the Bomb: Why Nuclear Weapons Programs Often Fail on Their Own – and Why Iran's Might, Too', *Foreign Affairs* (May/June 2012).
[7] For a thoughtful overview, see Steven Pinker, *The Better Angels of Our Nature: The Decline of Violence in History and its Causes* (London: Allen Lane, 2011), especially Chapters 5 and 6. Also see Andrew Mack et al., *Human Security Report 2009/10: The Causes of Peace and the Shrinking Costs of War* (New York: Oxford University Press, 2011).

strength and create new empires have been at the root of many past conflicts. In the new world order that was created after the Second World War, however, attempts to change borders have been much more limited than in the past, and rarely successful. Some of the most prominent exceptions, such as the invasions of South Korea, Kuwait and East Timor, were all reversed through concerted international action. Others – such as the secession of Kosovo from Serbia in the aftermath of NATO military action, and the Russia-sponsored secession of South Ossetia and Abkhazia from Georgia – remain deeply contested. After the dissolution of Europe's empires in the 1950s and 1960s, the number of arbitrary and disputable borders has increased sharply. However, attempts to resolve these conflicts by force have remained relatively limited, thereby helping to strengthen the Long Peace of the 'post-war' period.

Nuclear weapons may not have been the main force behind the consolidation of the border stability norm; but the strengthening of this norm has probably played a role in reducing proliferation pressures, helping to reassure most states that their territorial integrity is not under threat. Conversely, when this integrity has been threatened, new nuclear-weapons programmes have often followed. India's commitment to a nuclear-weapons programme was strengthened by the humiliation of defeat by China in the short mountain war of 1962. Pakistan made the decision to launch its own nuclear programme after the Indian invasion of its eastern half in 1971, which resulted in the establishment of Bangladesh. Iranian determination to acquire a military nuclear capability is often seen to be rooted in its bitter experience in its 1980–88 war, when it was left to defend itself against a clear act of aggression, designed to annex the most oil-rich parts of its territory to Saddam Hussein's Iraq.

Towards a Faustian Ending
While the 'war optimists' are right to point to overall trends towards a more pacific world, however, these examples – and others – suggest that it is too early to call time on war. Nuclear weapons are not all that stands between humanity and a return to great power conflict: wider political and social trends are also playing a powerful pacifying role in world politics. Nevertheless, when it comes to nuclear war, a small risk of conflict must still be taken seriously. That is why 'deterrence pessimists' emphasise that the theory of nuclear deterrence could turn out to be a Faustian bargain. Even if nuclear weapons contributed to peace in the early days of the Cold War, their continuing existence in the military arsenals of many states poses an ever-present risk to international security.

Deterrence pessimism is entirely compatible with the belief, strongly held by members of the US strategic nuclear community, that the possession of, and preparedness to use, nuclear weapons is nevertheless less risky than any conceivable non-nuclear alternative. Since nuclear weapons cannot realistically be abolished, they argue, the US must prepare nuclear war-fighting strategies that allow it to minimise damage in the event that deterrence fails. This in turn has meant that the US needs to invest heavily in capabilities – such as accurate long-range (nuclear and conventional) missiles, missile defences and civil defence – that can support such a strategy.[8]

The deliberate manipulation of nuclear risks is widely believed to be an indispensable part of the effectiveness of nuclear deterrence during a crisis. Yet further, and less easily predictable, risks can arise as a result of the personal characteristics and inter-personal dynamics of leaders, on whose shoulders a nuclear crisis places enormous responsibilities. Khrushchev's emotional and risk-taking approach to policy heightened the dangers of war in both the Berlin and Cuban crises, as did his vulnerability to pressure from more hawkish allies (especially Mao Zedong) and domestic rivals. For his part, Kennedy was taking a cocktail of pills and injections (including amphetamines and steroids), designed to offset his chronic back pain, Addison's disease and assorted other ailments. These may have contributed to his lacklustre performance at the Vienna summit, which in turn encouraged Khrushchev's risk-taking propensities.[9]

Nor was the confrontation over the future of Berlin the only time during the Cold War in which there was a real risk that nuclear weapons might have been used. Little more than a year later, Khrushchev's decision to deploy Soviet nuclear missiles in Cuba generated a further escalation in tension, which brought the world as close to nuclear war as it may ever have been. As Richard Holbrooke observed in his review of Michael Dobbs's 2008 account of the Cuban crisis:[10]

> [I]t is hard to read this book without thinking about what would have happened if the current … [George W Bush] administration had faced such a situation – real weapons of mass destruction only 90 miles from Florida; the Pentagon urging 'surgical' air attacks followed by an invasion; threatening letters from the leader of a real superpower and senators calling the president 'weak' just weeks before a midterm

[8] For an early example of this argument, see Colin S Gray and Keith Payne, 'Victory is Possible', *Foreign Policy* (Summer 1980), pp. 14–27, in which they argued that 'an intelligent United States offensive [nuclear] strategy, wedded to homeland defenses, should reduce U.S. casualties to approximately 20 million … a combination of counterforce offensive targeting, civil defense, and ballistic missile and air defense should hold U.S. casualties down to a level compatible with national survival and recovery.'

[9] *Ibid.*, pp. 212–14. Also see David Owen, *In Sickness and In Power: Illness in Heads of Government during the Last 100 Years* (London: Methuen Publishing Ltd, 2008), pp. 164–77.

[10] Richard Holbrooke, 'Real W.M.D.s', *New York Times*, 22 June 2008, reviewing Michael Dobbs, *Kennedy, Khrushchev, and Castro on the Brink of Nuclear War* (New York: Alfred A Knopf, 2008).

congressional election . . . it is not unreasonable to assume that the team that invaded Iraq would have attacked Cuba. And, if Dobbs is right, Cuba and the Soviet Union would have fought back, perhaps launching some of the missiles already in place.

Subsequent crises, both in the Middle East (the 1967 and 1973 Arab-Israeli wars) and in Europe (notably the 1983 'Able Archer' incident) also involved fears of nuclear escalation. Furthermore, it is too early to say that war between India and Pakistan has become impossible, simply because they now both have nuclear arsenals. The 1999 Kargil conflict, while relatively limited in scope, should add further caution in this regard. Nuclear pessimists also point to the Middle East, where they view with alarm the prospect that Iran could acquire nuclear weapons, possibly triggering a regional cascade of proliferation.

The lesson that nuclear pessimists draw, from both the Cold War and subsequent proliferation, is that there is no such thing as zero risk where nuclear weapons are involved. The risk that events could get 'out of hand', and trigger a descent into a scale of extreme violence never before experienced, is not a side-effect of a policy based on threats to use nuclear weapons: it is a necessary ingredient of a credible policy of nuclear deterrence.

Efforts to manipulate this risk so as to prevent war, yet never to precipitate it, have taxed even the wisest and most well-informed leaders. However, most decision-makers, schooled in the art of domestic politics and often with little understanding of international affairs, are far from suited to the responsibilities that possession of nuclear weapons confers.[11] Every effort needs to be made to support them in this role, and to minimise the risk that human frailty could lead to catastrophic outcomes. In particular, minimising the role of nuclear weapons in security doctrine will reduce the frequency with which those leaders will face pressure to seriously consider their use. Nevertheless, as long as nuclear weapons exist – and perhaps even after they have gone – humanity will have to live with the risk that they might one day be used.

Morality and Consequences

Since nuclear weapons have never been used since 1945, there is no sure way of assessing whether the annual probability of nuclear war over the next two decades is vanishingly low (say less than one in a thousand per

---

[11] Scott Sagan has emphasised the important role that organisational and bureaucratic factors (for example, in relation to the transmission and distortion of information) can play in increasing the possibility of nuclear escalation in a crisis. Scott D Sagan, *The Limits of Safety: Organizations, Accidents and Nuclear Weapons* (Princeton, NJ: Princeton University Press, 1995).

year), or just low (one in a hundred). Such an event could be a 'black swan' event, judged so improbable as not to have been the subject of serious consideration or planning.[12] Alternatively, it could involve one of the many scenarios for nuclear use that are the subject of day-to-day nuclear planning and preparation, but which those involved hope never become reality.

How can decision-makers navigate the terrible moral dilemmas that this situation produces? Even in conditions of 'normal' war, attempts to impose a decision-making matrix dominated by 'rational' cost-benefit analysis and consequentialism will fail to capture all the uncertainties and emotions that a descent into large-scale violence involves.

This is why the normative dimension of the nuclear debate is so important. Since the early days of the nuclear age, their destructive power ensured that nuclear weapons were seen as being in a class apart, along with other 'weapons of mass destruction'.[13] In contrast to chemical and biological weapons, their possession by those major powers which had already tested weapons by 1968 was not made illegal. Indeed, the NPT specifically recognised that these five states (the 'N5') possessed nuclear weapons, while requiring them to pursue disarmament negotiations in good faith. Three other nuclear-armed states – India, Pakistan and Israel – remain outside the treaty, but are no longer under significant pressure (at least from the N5) to join it as non-nuclear-weapon states. A ninth state, North Korea, has been outside the NPT since 2003, and therefore legally tested nuclear devices in 2006 and 2009.

While possession remains legal for this group of five states, however, the norm against the use of these weapons has grown steadily since the early years of the nuclear age. For much of the early part of the Cold War, until the dual crises of Berlin and Cuba and even beyond, US and Soviet war plans envisaged the early, and massive, use of nuclear weapons against each other should war between them break out. Indeed, when the Kennedy Administration entered office in 1961, its leading members were shocked to find that the main plan for the use of nuclear weapons in war with the Soviet Union was to launch a massive attack on military and civilian targets in the Soviet Union and its allies, a plan that would be likely to cause 175 million deaths in the Soviet Union and China alone.[14]

---

[12] Nassim Nicholas Taleb, *The Black Swan: The Impact of the Highly Improbable* (London: Penguin Books, 2008). 'Black swan theory' refers to unexpected events of large magnitude and consequence and their dominant role in history. Taleb argues that such events, considered extreme outliers, collectively play vastly larger roles than regular occurrences.

[13] Malcolm Chalmers, 'Nuclear Narratives: Reflections on Declaratory Policy', RUSI Whitehall Report, 1–10, 2010, p. 10.

[14] Fred Kaplan, *The Wizards of Armageddon* (New York: Simon and Schuster, 1983), p. 269.

Since that time, however, the inhibition against nuclear use, or even against explicit threats of use, has deepened markedly.[15] One of the most important manifestations of this trend has been the development of a non-testing norm. Starting with US and Soviet agreement to the Partial Test Ban Treaty in 1963, and through the successful negotiation of the CTBT (Comprehensive Test Ban Treaty) in 1996, the international acceptability of nuclear testing has continued to decline. The treaty has still not entered into force, and only three of the seven established nuclear-armed states (France, Russia and the UK) have completed the ratification process. Nevertheless, none of these states have tested a weapon since the CTBT opened for signature, with the exception of India and Pakistan, which conducted their first, and so far only, series of tests a few months later, in May 1998. The use, or even testing, of nuclear weapons is therefore increasingly viewed as something separate from 'normal' armed conflict, to which responsible nuclear powers would only resort in the most extreme circumstances. NATO's Strategic Concept, for example, concludes that 'the circumstances in which any use of nuclear weapons might have to be contemplated are extremely remote'.[16] The US's 2010 Nuclear Posture Review states that its goal is to create the conditions for the adoption of a 'sole purpose' posture, in which it would give up altogether any options for nuclear first use. China insists that the only role for its nuclear weapons is as a means for deterring the use of nuclear weapons against it by others.

The inhibitions against the use of nuclear weapons by the major powers now appear to have increasingly deep ethical foundations. Nuclear weapons gain their unique deterrent value, it is argued, by being able to ensure unprecedented levels of destruction within a period of only a few days. Yet it is this very quality that also makes their use so morally repugnant. The certitude that dreadful consequences will follow strips away the fog of uncertainty that can sometimes allow leaders to initiate conventional conflict in the (often mistaken) belief that the costs involved will be limited.

---

[15] Nina Tannenwald, *The Nuclear Taboo: The United States and the Non-Use of Nuclear Weapons Since 1945* (Cambridge: Cambridge University Press, 2007) argues for the existence of a 'taboo' against nuclear use in the US, which includes a perception that only 'barbarians' would use them (see p. 16). Others argue that, given continuing preparation for use by nuclear-armed states in some circumstances, non-use can be better characterised as a 'tradition'. T V Paul, *The Tradition of Non-Use of Nuclear Weapons* (Stanford, CA: Stanford University Press, 2009), p. 8, also argues that, if non-use were indeed a commonly accepted taboo, one might expect greater support for use to be outlawed in international law (a treatment applied to other taboo activities, such as torture and slavery).
[16] NATO, 'Strategic Concept for the Defence and Security of the Members of the North Atlantic Alliance', November 2010, para. 17.

In an epoch of relative peace, with the last world war having finished before any of the heads of government of today's major powers were born, the moral restraints on nuclear use are significantly higher than in the immediate post-war period. The US nuclear bombings of Hiroshima and Nagasaki in August 1945 were the culmination of one of the most violent and inhumane wars of modern history. Despite widespread ethical concerns, indiscriminate attacks on urban population centres became a central part of both Allied and Axis war efforts. Ethical constraints on civilian targeting (among the Western Allies) loosened as the war progressed, so that by 1945 the use of atomic bombs did not seem as big a step as it would now.

This attitude – that nuclear weapons were just a larger weapon, and posed no unique moral challenges – still shaped attitudes in the US and Soviet Union into the 1950s and early 1960s, a period characterised by a series of nuclearised crises. However, as the distance from 1945 has lengthened, war aversion – and aversion to nuclear war in particular – has strengthened, further undermining the credibility of military doctrines based on early nuclear use.

From the start of the nuclear age, normative prohibitions against nuclear weapons have been issued by religious leaders of every faith. The Pope continues to call for the elimination of nuclear weapons, calling them a 'source of tension and mistrust' on the 65th anniversary of the bombings of Hiroshima and Nagasaki in 2010. The importance of normative pressure against nuclear weapons is also reflected in the pronouncements of Iran's Supreme Leader Ayatollah Khamenei, who recently stated that possession or use of nuclear weapons by Iran (though not the pursuit of technological advances with possible military applications) would be a 'grave sin' against Islam.[17] In the last analysis, none of these religious prohibitions have been enough in themselves to prevent countries from acquiring, or indeed using, nuclear weapons if it is felt to be in their interests to do so. However, they do have a profound effect on how those interests are themselves created, narrowing the circumstances in which leaders would seriously consider their use; and they solidify the very clear distinction – the 'nuclear threshold' – that exists between the use of nuclear weapons and the waging of war with conventional weapons.

As previously discussed, nuclear restraint has been reinforced by the broader decline in violence since 1945, both within and between major powers, and by the strong norms against chemical and biological weapons. Tolerance for casualties, whether to a state's own forces or 'collateral damage' to non-combatants, in those limited wars that have taken place seems to be declining over time; and these broader trends have not been

---

[17] Colin H Kahl, 'Before Attacking Iran, Israel Should Learn from its 1981 Strike on Iraq', *Washington Post*, 2 March 2012.

confined to the Western democracies. Other major powers – such as China, India, Russia, Brazil and Indonesia – have seen a marked decline in levels of domestic repression since the first post-1945 decades; and none of these states – which are, respectively, the five largest non-OECD economies – have been involved in large-scale inter-state wars since the end of the Cold War. Awareness of the risk that any major war could be nuclearised may have contributed to this Long Peace. However, the roots appear deeper, based both on new conceptions of national interest in a much more integrated world economy, together with a widespread, albeit not universal, rejection of the militarist ideologies that had predominated in the first half of the twentieth century.

It is therefore difficult to imagine a credible scenario for an all-out war between major powers over the next decade; but, such a threat did exist in the Cold War, when ideological antagonism, uncertainty over local balances of military forces, and the difficulties of managing weaker allies (such as East Germany, Cuba and Israel) all contributed to the risks of nuclear war. While the US and allied powers continue to hedge against the re-emergence of such a possibility in the long term, however, none of the other major powers have either the material resources or the level of domestic authoritarianism that would be necessary to turn this hypothetical risk into a credible threat at present. Nevertheless, shifts in the balance of conventional military power, or erosion in the credibility of existing alliance commitments, might increase the risks of miscalculation in a future political crisis.

Alongside the requirement to hedge against long-term deterioration of major power relations, however, a more immediate concern is how to deal with regimes that – albeit on a much smaller scale – bear a closer resemblance to the Soviet Union or Hitler's Germany than do any of today's major powers. Such regimes – such as North Korea – lack the economic or military strength of their historical role models; but they share a willingness to resort to extreme violence, both internally and externally, and their very weakness could make their attempts to acquire nuclear weapons more dangerous. The pressure for them to do so may have been heightened by the increased willingness of the US and its allies to intervene militarily in order to overthrow what they see as particularly odious regimes.

Such states may even be willing to supply nuclear material or devices to non-state allies, with all the uncertainties and risks that this would involve. In line with this new focus on the nuclear threats posed by rogue states and non-state actors, the 2010 US Nuclear Posture Review identified nuclear terrorism and proliferation as the most pressing nuclear threats that the US and the international community face. While 'the threat of global nuclear war has become remote', it argued, 'the risk of nuclear attack has increased.'[18]

The Case for Low Numbers

Human Frailty
In his work on the obsolescence of major war, John Mueller has argued that, given all the structural factors supporting peace between the major powers in the early twentieth century, the Second World War should never have happened. It would not have happened, he suggests, had Hitler not become leader of the National Socialist Party, and then of Germany: 'major war in Europe could in all probability have been prevented if at any time Adolf Hitler had gotten in the way of a lethal germ, a well-placed bullet, or a speeding truck.'[19]

One can equally imagine a future historian reflecting that mutual interest and the logic of deterrence should have avoided a 2025 nuclear war between India and Pakistan, or Israel and Iran, had it not been for the fateful flaws of an especially charismatic leader in one of these countries. As Thérèse Delpech warned shortly before her own death:[20]

> The problem was, and still is, the conjunction of immensely destructive weapons with leaders as they have always been – prudent or trigger-happy, determined or hesitant, courageous or cowardly, intelligent or dumb.

The experiences of the Berlin and Cuban crises also suggest that, even when leaders want to avoid nuclear war, they do not, and importantly cannot be seen to, prefer this objective at all costs. As Marc Trachtenberg suggests:[21]

> [E]ach side [in a nuclear rivalry] would be afraid of escalation, but each side would in the final analysis also be willing to run a certain risk, knowing that its adversary was also worried about what would happen if things got out of hand, and that an unwillingness to run any risk at all would remove that element of restraint and give the adversary too free a hand.

---

[18] US Department of Defense, 'Nuclear Posture Review Report 2010', April 2010, p. iv.
[19] John E Mueller, *Retreat from Doomsday: The Obsolescence of Major War* (New York: Basic Books, 1989), p. 69.
[20] Thérèse Delpech, *Nuclear Deterrence in the 21st Century: Lessons from the Cold War for a New Era of Strategic Piracy* (Santa Monica, CA: RAND Corporation, 2012), p. 37.
[21] Marc Trachtenberg, 'Proliferation Revisited', as quoted in Shashank Joshi, 'Is a Nuclear Iran as Dangerous as We Think?', *RUSI.org*, 27 February 2012.

President Kennedy and Premier Khrushchev both faced pressure to take a tougher line from important domestic constituents and from key allies. Even as they sought to avoid nuclear war, therefore, they also sought to manipulate the fear of such a conflict in order to coerce the other to make concessions. Such behaviour was consistent with the teachings of key deterrence thinkers such as Thomas Schelling:[22]

> Violence, especially war, is a confused and uncertain activity, highly unpredictable, depending on decisions made by fallible human beings organised into imperfect governments, depending on fallible communications and warning systems and on the untested performance of people and equipment. It is furthermore a hotheaded activity, in which commitments and reputations can develop a momentum of their own.

Concerns that the manipulation of threats could, in times of crisis, lead to levels of violence that spiral out of control are instinctively plausible when the possibility of proliferation in other states (such as Iran or North Korea) is contemplated. The long absence of nuclear war between more established nuclear-weapon states, by contrast, has led to a widespread assumption that deterrence between them has become so 'mature' that the risks are much smaller. Yet it is possible to imagine Russia, China or the US confronting a crisis in which its leaders would be unable to survive politically (and perhaps even personally) without being seen to be taking a firm line against a perceived aggression by another nuclear-armed state. Some leaders, for both personal and national cultural reasons, may be more likely to take such risks than others. As Schelling suggests:[23]

> A government that is obliged to appear responsible in its foreign policy can hardly cultivate forever the appearance of impetuosity on the most important decisions in its care...Deterrent threats are a matter of resolve, impetuosity, plain obstinacy, or, as the anarchist put it, sheer character. It is not easy to change our character; and becoming fanatic or impetuous would be a high price to pay for making our threats convincing.

Yet the differences between 'immature' and 'mature' powers may not be as great as this dichotomy suggests. Even in the most long-established nuclear powers, leaders during a period of international crisis could still be tempted to enter 'commitment traps' in order to persuade an opponent that escalation would occur if it persisted with a particular, unacceptable course of action. For example, as Scott Sagan argues, attempts to manipulate the

---

[22] Thomas C Schelling, *Arms and Influence* (New Haven: Yale University Press, 1966), p. 93.
[23] *Ibid.*, pp. 40–42. I am indebted to Shashank Joshi for this reference.

possible use of nuclear weapons in order to deter the use of chemical and biological weapons by others could mean that, if the use of chemical or biological weapons did take place, 'a president would feel increased pressure to use nuclear weapons to maintain his or her domestic reputation and America's international reputation for honouring its commitments.'[24] Precisely because of this risk, Sagan argues that the US, like China, should be prepared to pledge never to use nuclear weapons first in a conflict. For, even if such a pledge may not be entirely credible to an opponent in all circumstances, it avoids creating a domestic expectation for a nuclear response, not least amongst US military planners and leaders.

The very length of time that has now elapsed without a major nuclear crisis may itself be a problem: because the possibility of nuclear crisis is seen as increasingly remote, there is a danger that ensuring the safety and security of nuclear arsenals has become an increasingly less attractive task for the military personnel involved. This tendency towards careless practices may be increased in societies where there is an excessive cult of military secrecy.

The disastrous consequences of complacent behaviour on the part of unaccountable bureaucracies were seen vividly in the Fukushima nuclear disaster of 2011. The possibility of an even more serious set of events involving nuclear weapons, in one of the nine states that now possess them, cannot be ruled out. As Charles Perrow argues in his work on 'normal accidents', high-risk accidents are more likely in systems characterised by 'interactive complexity and tight coupling'. Nuclear deterrent relationships in a period of crisis would have these very features.[25]

A Global Catastrophe

If the use of nuclear weapons in any of these various ways is a real and significant possibility, however, there must also be a strong case for adopting measures that could reduce the damage.

Although there is an orders-of-magnitude difference between the effects of a nuclear exchange involving tens of nuclear weapons and one involving the global destruction that a superpower conflict during the Cold War would probably have triggered, even the former would be a disaster of unparalleled dimensions. A nuclear war that resulted in twenty Hiroshima-yield ground-burst nuclear explosions in the major cities of Russia or China could be a catastrophe comparable in scale to the Second World War for

---

[24] Scott D Sagan, 'The Case for No First Use', *Survival* (Vol. 51, No. 3, June–July 2009), p. 170.
[25] Charles Perrow, *Normal Accidents: Living with High-Risk Technologies* (Princeton, NJ: Princeton University Press, 1984). Also see Sagan, *The Limits of Safety*.

those countries, both in terms of total casualties and economic and social disruption.

Countries whose territory was not ravaged by that war – such as the US and India – would face a disaster beyond any recent historical comparison (except perhaps for the Civil War for the US) if they were to suffer a similar attack. Medium-sized countries, such as the UK or Iran, could suffer hundreds of thousands of fatalities even if only one or two explosions were to take place in urban centres; and smaller states with concentrated populations – such as Israel – would find it difficult to survive as viable political units after such a 'small-scale' nuclear attack.

A nuclear war, even if it involved 'only' twenty or thirty attacks on the world's major cities, would create such high levels of political, social and economic disruption, and so suddenly, that many more could die in the consequent turmoil. Idealists might hope that such a shock would, at last, lead to unstoppable citizen pressure for global disarmament. Depending on why such a war had been fought and ended, however, it might instead lead to a period of rapid military remobilisation and rearming as 'victim' states – a status that many might claim – sought protection and revenge.

Not All Nuclear Wars are the Same
Yet such a war would not be the end of the world. It would not prevent politically stable states – such as the UK, India or China – from recovering and rebuilding, as countries have done after terrible, and longer, wars in the past. After the air-burst attack on Nagasaki in 1945, 'many modern buildings of steel and concrete survived . . . railroad tracks, streets and underground water lines were largely undamaged. Electrical service was restored within one day, railroad and trolley service within two, telephone service within seven, and the debris was largely cleared up within two weeks.'[26] Many more Japanese died as a result of the sustained conventional bombing campaign than as a result of the two atomic bombs used on Hiroshima and Nagasaki.

Plans for large-scale nuclear exchanges using the arsenals available to the US and the Soviet Union at the peak of the Cold War, in contrast, would have resulted in much higher levels of casualties. Both government and non-government studies in the 1980s estimated the effects of a large-scale Soviet nuclear attack on the UK, involving the use of up to 350 warheads, with a total yield of around 200 megatons, on a range of military, industrial and civilian targets across the country. The resulting devastation would have led (according to estimates by independent scientists) to total casualties as high as 48 million (80 per cent of the

---

[26] John E Mueller, *Atomic Obsession*, p. 10.

population), with every major industrial and government facility destroyed. The only large areas left relatively free from blast effects would have been areas with low populations and few targets, such as the Scottish Highlands and Borders, together with central and northern parts of Wales.[27]

Even remote areas such as these, together with regions and countries that had not been directly targeted, would also have suffered from the wider environmental effects of a global nuclear war.

Climatic Consequences of Limited Nuclear War

During the 1980s, scientists pointed to a world-wide 'nuclear winter' as one of the probable consequences of a large-scale nuclear war.[28] Such an effect, analysts argued, would be created when the smoke from the fires created by nuclear attacks on cities and industrial facilities is pushed into the upper atmosphere, spreading globally and creating cold and dark climatic conditions on the surface that could last for several years.[29] Others were more cautious, pointing to the many scientific uncertainties involved, and arguing that the effects would be more modest (though far from non-existent).[30]

There is also a distinct possibility that a nuclear war involving no more than a fraction of the weapons currently in global arsenals, especially if these are aimed at cities or industrial facilities, could still produce global environmental effects that could have considerable consequences for food production worldwide. It is also clear that the risk of a substantial effect of this kind is greater as the number of weapons involved is increased. One recent study, using climate models that are more advanced than those available in the 1980s, has estimated that even a relatively small nuclear war (involving fifty kiloton-range weapons dropped on industrial centres in both India and Pakistan) could produce 5 million tonnes of black smoke, enough to produce a global average cooling of about 1.25°C, lasting for several years.[31]

---

[27] Stan Openshaw, Philip Steadman and Owen Greene, *Doomsday: Britain after Nuclear Attack* (Oxford: Blackwell, 1983), especially pp. 92, 214.

[28] For recent contributions to the nuclear winter literature, see Alan Robock, Luke Roman and Georgiy L Stenchikov, 'Nuclear Winter Revisited with a Modern Climate Model and Current Nuclear Arsenals: Still Catastrophic Consequences', *Journal of Geophysical Research* (Vol. 112, D13107, 2007); Steven Starr, 'Catastrophic Climate Consequences of Nuclear Conflict', paper prepared for the International Commission on Nuclear Nonproliferation and Disarmament, October 2009; Alan Robock, 'Nuclear Winter is a Real and Present Danger', *Nature* (Vol. 473, 19 May 2012), pp. 275–77.

[29] Alan Robock, 'Nuclear Winter', *Climate Change* (No. 1, May/June 2010).

[30] US National Academy of Sciences, *The Effects on the Atmosphere of a Major Nuclear Exchange* (Washington, DC: National Academy Press, 1985).

[31] Alan Robock, 'Nuclear Winter is a Real and Present Danger', p. 276.

It is surprising, given both the attention given to this phenomenon in the 1980s and the considerable resources being devoted to modelling greenhouse-gas-generated climate change, that these studies have not been subjected to more rigorous peer review. Until the hypothesis of a nuclear winter is refuted, however, the risk that it could take place surely suggests a further benefit from reducing global nuclear stockpiles to much lower levels.

For some, an examination of the relative effects of different levels of nuclear conflict risks being seen as an effort to distinguish between the horrors of one sort of nuclear war and another, in the process legitimising 'safer' forms of conflict. Unfortunately, however, nuclear war is both thinkable and possible, and will remain so for as long as nuclear weapons are part of the deterrent strategies of most of the world's major states (and perhaps even beyond that point). Responsible policy-makers must do all they can to reduce the likelihood that any of these weapons would ever be used. However, they also need to do what they can to minimise the damage that might take place should such a conflict ever take place. This suggests that policy-makers should seek to ensure that numbers of operationally available nuclear weapons are reduced as quickly as possible. It may also suggest, for example, paying particular attention to reducing the yield of deployed weapons in the arsenals of the most established nuclear-weapon states, as well as persuading India and Pakistan not to move towards the replacement of existing low-yield weapons with larger-yield thermonuclear weapons.

Non-State Actors and Low Numbers

The risk that nuclear weapons could be used in a conflict between states is the most serious one that the world faces, given the number and destructive power of the weapons available. However, there is also growing concern that nuclear weapons, or associated fissile material, could fall into the hands of terrorist or other non-state actors. Most recently, this concern was reflected in President Barack Obama's success in persuading other world leaders to establish a regular Nuclear Security Summit, the second of which took place in South Korea in March 2012.

The possibility that nuclear weapons could be threatened or used in the event of civil conflict within a nuclear-armed state (such as Pakistan or China) can also not be entirely dismissed. If the security forces in such a state were to splinter or disintegrate, control over nuclear forces could become a bargaining chip.[32] Efforts to conceal such forces, not least from

---

[32] On the nuclear dimension of Algeria's separation from France, see Bruno Tertrais, 'A "Nuclear Coup"? France, the Algerian War and the April 1961 Nuclear Test', <http://www.npolicy.org/article_file/A_Nuclear_Coup-France_the_Algerian_War_and_the_April_1961_Nuclear_Test.pdf>, accessed 26 July 2012.

US efforts to secure them, could make them less secure and perhaps more likely to be kept in a higher state of readiness. If Iraq, Libya and Syria had possessed nuclear weapons during their recent civil wars, such concerns would have been at the top of the international agenda. In future, Pakistan and North Korea are the obvious cases in which a civil conflict might have a nuclear dimension.

III. THE LOGIC OF NUCLEAR RESTRAINT

The purpose of this chapter is to discuss the broad conditions in which nuclear restraint at low numbers could contribute to international security, establishing the principles and definitions upon which more detailed policy implications are then developed in the next chapter.

Until all nuclear-armed states are willing to agree to abolish their nuclear weapons together, nuclear restraint at low numbers may be the best way to minimise, as far as possible, the risks of nuclear conflict. If political circumstances between the major powers improve sufficiently, nuclear restraint at low numbers might one day provide a jumping-off point from which to move to nuclear abolition more rapidly, and with greater confidence than in a strictly time-bound framework. More likely, and perhaps for some decades, it could also provide a path through which those states which currently possess nuclear capabilities maintain a small arsenal, but within a framework that further restricts their role and reduces the potential for arms racing.

A Long and Winding Road

The US's 2010 Nuclear Posture Review confirmed President Obama's commitment, first made in his April 2009 speech in Prague, to 'seek the peace and security of a world without nuclear weapons'. While recognising that such an objective might not be achieved in his lifetime, he made clear his determination to take concrete steps towards this goal, 'including reducing the number of nuclear weapons and their role in US national security strategy'.[1]

President Obama is not the first US president to set this objective, as pointed out by James Miller, then the principal deputy under-secretary of defense for policy: 'Every President since the nuclear age began has advocated the eventual elimination of nuclear weapons with one

---

[1] US Department of Defense, 'Nuclear Posture Review Report 2010', April 2010, p. iii.

exception. That was George W Bush. Every President since Truman has advocated that as a goal. President Obama, I think, is therefore not unique in that goal.'[2] Nor was this only a matter of campaigning rhetoric. In 1977, President-elect Carter asked the Joint Chiefs for a study of a minimum nuclear posture consisting of 200–50 submarine-launched warheads.[3] His immediate successor, President Reagan, told President Gorbachev that 'it would be fine with me if we eliminated all nuclear weapons', and made radical proposals for putting this into practice.[4] Even some of those who were sceptical of Reagan's commitment during the Cold War – such as Henry Kissinger – joined his former Secretary of State George Shultz (who accompanied Reagan at Reykjavik) in calling for a 'world free of nuclear weapons' in a widely circulated opinion piece in the *Wall Street Journal* in January 2007.[5]

This aspiration has been shared by political leaders and a large element of informed public opinion in many of the US's closest allies, as well as in non-aligned states. In May 2007, UK Foreign Secretary Margaret Beckett committed the UK to take a leading role in nuclear disarmament efforts, arguing that:[6]

> If we allow our efforts on disarmament to slacken, if we allow ourselves to take the non-proliferation consensus for granted, the nuclear shadow that hangs over us will lengthen and it will deepen. And it may, one day, blot out the light for good.

In December 2009, the International Commission on Nuclear Non-proliferation and Disarmament, established by the governments of Australia and Japan, published its final report, which argued for strong support for the 'continued delegitimisation of nuclear weapons, and the ultimate achievement of a completely nuclear weapon free world'.[7]

---

[2] 'Hearing Before the Subcommittee on Strategic Forces of the Committee on Armed Services, United States Senate, May 4, 2011', p. 6, <http://www.fas.org/irp/congress/2011_hr/newstart.pdf>, accessed 8 August 2012.

[3] Jeffrey G Lewis, 'Minimum Deterrence', New America Foundation, <http://www.newamerica.net/publications/articles/2008/minimum_deterrence_7552>, accessed 8 August 2012.

[4] Quoted in Philip Taubman, *The Partnership: Five Cold Warriors and Their Quest to Ban the Bomb* (New York: Harper Collins, 2012), p. 256.

[5] George P Shultz, William J Perry, Henry A Kissinger and Sam Nunn, 'A World Free of Nuclear Weapons', *Wall Street Journal*, 4 January 2007.

[6] Foreign Secretary Margaret Beckett, presentation given to Carnegie Non-Proliferation Conference, Washington, DC, 25 June 2007, <http://www.nuclearsecurityproject.org/publications/beckett-a-world-free-of-nuclear-weapons>, accessed 8 August 2012.

[7] International Commission on Nuclear Non-proliferation and Disarmament, 'Eliminating Nuclear Threats: A Practical Agenda for Global Policymakers', December 2009.

Even with the strong personal support of the US president, however, it has not been easy to make progress on the nuclear disarmament agenda. There were early successes. The UN Security Council summit in September 2009, presided over by President Obama, called for fresh momentum in nuclear disarmament efforts. Obama himself argued that 'we must never stop until we see the day that nuclear arms are banished from the face of the earth.'[8] In April 2010, Obama signed the New START Treaty with President Dmitry Medvedev of Russia, committing the two countries to reductions in their arsenals of deployed strategic missiles and warheads. In the same month, the US also convened the first Nuclear Security Summit in Washington DC, focusing international attention on a hitherto-neglected aspect of nuclear danger. Furthermore, the US's more supportive approach to nuclear disarmament played an important role in creating the conditions for a successful conclusion to the NPT review conference in May 2010, which was able to adopt unanimously a programme of action for the next five years.

Yet resistance to President Obama's disarmament agenda has also been evident, both within the US itself and from other Nuclear-Weapon States less keen on his 'vision' of a nuclear-free world. In order to gain Senate ratification of the New START Treaty in December 2010 (by only four votes more than the two-thirds required), the administration was obliged to promise significant new investments in nuclear infrastructure. Sustained efforts to reach agreement with Russia over a shared missile defence architecture for Europe proved fruitless, calling into question the durability of the 'reset' in relations between the two countries, and indeed between NATO and Russia. Furthermore, after the difficulties involved with New START, the administration postponed making a renewed effort to obtain Senate ratification of the CTBT, signed by the US in 1996.

Similarly, efforts by Germany and some other NATO member states to contribute to the Obama vision, by making further reductions in US nuclear weapons based in Europe, faced fierce resistance from France and some Central European NATO members. The NATO Deterrence and Defence Posture Review (DDPR), convened primarily to resolve this issue, essentially endorsed the status quo in its report to the NATO summit in Chicago in May 2012, with its main concern being that a withdrawal, especially in the absence of Russian reciprocation, would be seen as symbolising a weakening of Alliance cohesion. There was also concern at the proposed ending of 'nuclear-sharing' arrangements, through which non-nuclear states (such as Germany, Italy and Turkey) maintain a

---

[8] UN Department of Public Information (SC/9746), 'Historic Summit of Security Council Pledges Support for Progress on Stalled Efforts to End Nuclear Weapons Proliferation', 24 September 2009, <http://www.un.org/News/Press/docs/2009/sc9746.doc>, accessed 8 August 2012.

capability to use their attack aircraft in a nuclear role, using US nuclear warheads stored in Europe.[9]

In an attempt to inject new momentum into the nuclear disarmament process, it has sometimes been proposed that a fixed timetable for the elimination of nuclear weapons should be agreed. At the third Special Session on Disarmament (SSOD III) in 1988, for example, Prime Minister Rajiv Gandhi of India spoke about a 'world free of nuclear weapons' and sought a 'binding commitment by all nations to eliminate nuclear weapons in stages, by the year 2010.'[10] Since December 2008, Global Zero, an international movement committed to nuclear disarmament, has gathered 400,000 signatures for 'a legally binding verifiable agreement, including all nations, to eliminate nuclear weapons by a date certain'.[11] Most remarkably, in 1986, President Reagan proposed to General Secretary Gorbachev at the Reykjavik summit that 'all nuclear explosive devices' should be eliminated by the end of a ten-year period.[12]

Proposals for a similar 'leap of faith' will continue to be a feature of the disarmament debate; and the ultimate objective of a world without nuclear weapons can help mobilise political support for a process that progressively reduces their relevance in international affairs. Yet the complex and tightly knit hold of nuclear weapons on the international body politic will not be loosened easily. At each stage, confidence has to be built amongst key states and populations that their security is improving, and political coalitions built to enable change to take place.

Beyond the Big Two

The road towards nuclear disarmament has been complicated, since the days of the Cold War, by the need to take into account the existence of at least eight nuclear-armed states (or nine, if North Korea is included). In 1986, when Reagan and Gorbachev agreed to eliminate all nuclear weapons by 1996, no mention was made of the need to consult (far less gain the agreement of) China, France, Israel and the UK. For almost four decades, the superpowers managed (or mismanaged) potentially nuclearised international crises – in Berlin and in Cuba, in the Middle

---

[9] For a discussion of possible ways to make progress on this issue, see George Perkovich, Malcolm Chalmers, Steve Pifer, Paul Schulte and Jaclyn Tandler, *Looking Beyond the Chicago Summit: Nuclear Weapons in Europe and the Future of NATO*, Carnegie Endowment, April 2012.
[10] Rekha Chakravarthi, 'India & Nuclear Disarmament: Chasing a Dream', CBRN South Asia Brief (No. 12, March 2009), <http://www.ipcs.org/pdf_file/issue/CBRNIB12-Rekha-Disarmament.pdf>, accessed 8 August 2012.
[11] See Global Zero, <http://www.globalzero.org/sign-declaration>, accessed 8 August 2012.
[12] Philip Taubman, *The Partnership*, p. 256.

East and in Vietnam – between themselves and those allies which were directly involved. Efforts to control existing nuclear arsenals were a solely bilateral affair, through the Strategic Arms Limitation Treaty (SALT) and the Anti-Ballistic Missile (ABM) Treaty. The other four nuclear-armed states were viewed, with the partial exception of China, primarily through the prism of their close alliance with the US.

Yet, a quarter of a century after Reykjavik, the Cold War is a receding memory. Global economic power has been shifting towards China and other large emerging powers, most of which have strongly independent foreign policies, and some of which (like China and India) also have nuclear weapons. Pakistan has become a nuclear-armed state, and the prospect of a nuclear Iran is getting closer. If proposals for nuclear restraint are to be relevant, they need to take account of this new distribution of power.

A Pragmatic Middle Way

The objective of nuclear restraint at low numbers can be seen, in policy terms, as what William Walker calls a 'pragmatic middle way' between the 'logics of armament and disarmament' that have coexisted since the start of the nuclear age. Walker argues that this 'logic of restraint' entails 'accepting the presence of nuclear weapons in the world "for the time being" whilst placing limits on their possession and usage, without unduly impeding either deterrence or the diffusion of nuclear materials and technologies for civil purposes'. He goes on to argue that: 'installing and embedding this logic and rendering it tolerable have lain at the heart of the problem and project of nuclear order.'[13]

A policy agenda that contends that it is both possible and desirable to achieve nuclear restraint at low numbers is most consistent with the analysis of international politics that was set out in Chapter II. We live in a world in which major states still prepare for the possibility of war with each other, in which there is no world government to enforce dispute resolution, and indeed in which the role of global institutions (especially but not only in relation to security) remains sharply circumscribed. In such a world, the logic of nuclear deterrence, derived from the mutual vulnerability of the major powers, cannot simply be discarded as irrelevant and meaningless; but nor can the existence of nuclear deterrent relationships, and the power of nuclear deterrent narratives, be a cause for complacency. The risks of nuclear use remain, and the risks of failing to deliver on promises of restraint are considerable, both in terms of the legitimacy of the non-proliferation regime and in the continuing possibility that nuclear weapons might one day be used.

---

[13] William Walker, *A Perpetual Menace: Nuclear Weapons and International Order* (Abingdon: Routledge, 2012), p. 5.

While nuclear deterrence and mutual vulnerability is a fragile basis on which to rest the future of international security, proposals for greater restraint at lower numbers would be unlikely to get far if states were only held back from their dreams of conquest by the threat of societal annihilation. However, we do not live in such a Hobbesian nightmare of 'all against all'. For reasons beyond the existence of nuclear weapons, there has been a clear and unambiguous overall trend since the 1940s towards more pacific international relations, even if the risks of war in some regions remain considerable. The prospects for war between the major powers, in particular, have remained low since 1990. Neither China nor Russia wants a major war, and neither seems prepared to take the sort of excessive risks in pursuit of revisionist political ends that might precipitate such a conflict. The world is more likely to have to live with an uncertain, and unpredictable, mixture of co-operation and competition between the major powers for some time to come.

These are not political conditions in which a rapid transition to nuclear abolition is remotely feasible; but even without a fundamental transformation in international relationships, it is possible to imagine that the major powers might be prepared to move towards greater mutual nuclear restraint. The primary obstacle to this is the continuing possession of massive nuclear stockpiles by the US and Russia. While neither country would choose to build such large arsenals today, both now find it difficult to make further deep reductions without the other also doing so. By combining deep reductions in their own forces with wider restraint between all the nuclear-armed powers, however, they could help to create a nuclear restraint regime that is more appropriate to today's relatively pacific international order, and pave the way for further reductions, should conditions allow.

Mutual nuclear restraint does not provide an answer to moral objections to the use, or threatened use, of nuclear weapons; but smaller arsenals are certainly no less moral than large arsenals. Some supporters of the US's current nuclear posture have suggested that it is more moral because it is based around counterforce targeting, and because it does not deliberately target civilian populations. However, the US has not given up the option of attacking military and political targets which are co-located with civilian populations, for example in cities; and, in any case, the fallout and wider environmental effects of a large-scale US counterforce strike on Russia or China would likely result in massive levels of civilian death. If near-total disarmament of an opponent could be achieved in a counterforce strike, this might reduce the civilian casualties suffered by one's own side; but the possession of and plans to use such a capability pose a severe threat of crisis instability, thereby increasing the risk that nuclear weapons might be used.

Deep reductions in US and Russian arsenals need not call into question the role of US nuclear weapons in deterring nuclear threats against American allies in Europe and Asia. Restraint at low numbers would not be compatible with the US retaining the current level of 200 'non-strategic' weapons in Europe. However, such a large number will not be required, or wanted, if both Russia and the US have reduced their total arsenals to levels in the low hundreds.

Nor will nuclear restraint at low numbers transform the dynamic of relations with states (such as Iran and North Korea) that are thought to be seeking a national nuclear-weapons capability. However, it might make a difference to international proliferation trends by helping to persuade the wider community of UN member states that the US and its allies are not the primary obstacle to making progress on fulfilling the commitment to nuclear disarmament made in Article VI of the NPT. Such partial moves towards nuclear disarmament might not change the perceptions of key nuclear-capable Non-Nuclear-Weapon States (such as Brazil and Turkey), which complain about the 'double standards' inherent in current arrangements. At a minimum, however, restraint by the nuclear-armed states will help to avoid the negative consequences that a future round of nuclear arms racing would have on proliferation. An intensification of US-China-India nuclear competition, by contrast, could make it more difficult in the long term to convince states such as South Korea and Japan to refrain from acquiring their own nuclear forces.

Finite Deterrence

One of the conditions for achieving nuclear restraint at low numbers, particularly for the US and Russia as they assess the acceptability of deep cuts, is whether they are prepared to adopt a doctrine of 'finite deterrence', similar to that already adopted by China, France and the UK.

In such a posture, the US and Russia, like the Small Three, would retain the ability to inflict unacceptable damage on a potential adversary in a retaliatory strike. This capability, it is argued, would prevent another nuclear-armed country from using its nuclear monopoly to extract political concessions in other areas (one of the fundamental reasons why states want nuclear weapons, either of their own or as part of a nuclear security guarantee from the US). However, it would be a 'finite' deterrent, insofar as force size would not be related to the size of the other states' nuclear forces, but to the level of capability necessary to inflict a certain level of retaliatory damage. Moreover, given the destructive power of even a single nuclear weapon, such a posture could be achieved by an ability to deliver only a small number of weapons on target in a second strike.

Capabilities to use nuclear weapons will never just cancel each other out. The 2010 US Nuclear Posture Review made clear that the 'fundamental role' of the US nuclear force was to deter the use of nuclear weapons against itself, its allies or its partners. It went on to issue a 'negative security assurance', making it clear that it would not 'use or threaten to use nuclear weapons against non-nuclear weapons states that are party to the NPT and in compliance with their non-proliferation obligations.'

The US's negative security assurance is welcome, both as a strengthening of reassurance to Non-Nuclear-Weapon States in an NPT context, and as a clear signal to military planners that other forms of response need to be prioritised. It is given added credibility by US conventional strength, which would provide many retaliatory options not available to other states. Nevertheless, no potential adversary could be confident that a US president will turn first to past negative security assurances for guidance in responding to a massive biological weapon attack on Washington or Los Angeles. Moreover, the US also made clear that this commitment did not apply to nuclear-armed states or to states (such as Iran) which the US deemed not to be in compliance with the NPT:[14]

> [In the case of countries not covered, there] remains a narrow range of contingencies in which U.S. nuclear weapons may still play a role in deterring a conventional or CBW attack against the United States or its allies and partners. The United States is therefore not prepared at the present time to adopt a universal policy that deterring nuclear attack is the sole purpose of nuclear weapons, but will work to establish conditions under which such a policy could be safely adopted.

Similarly, the possibility of a nuclear response could not be ruled out even if an adversary were to invade a nuclear-armed state with a declaratory policy of No First Use (such as China). Even if such an attack threatened only part of the victim's territory, it might be seen as so affecting the wider credibility of the state or alliance in question that it might be willing to risk nuclear war to prevent further aggression. This explains why the US was prepared to consider the use of nuclear weapons in response to a Soviet attempt to cut off access to West Berlin in 1961.[15] In general, however, the more limited the aggression, and the more other options for response (military or non-military) are available, the less credible nuclear threats will be.

By contrast, the threat of nuclear first use is more credible – not certain, but certainly possible – when the very survival of a state is in question and it has exhausted other alternatives for defence. The strategic and political cultures of all the world's major powers continue to be based

---

[14] US Department of Defense, 'Nuclear Posture Review Report 2010', p. viii.

[15] Frederick Kempe, *Berlin 1961: Kennedy, Khrushchev and the Most Dangerous Place on Earth* (New York: Berkley Books, 2011), pp. 442–43.

on their distinct, and deeply traumatic, national experiences in the Second World War. Three of the major powers – the Soviet Union, China and France – endured brutal occupation of large parts of their territory by enemies which, had they prevailed, would have threatened the lives of many millions and extinguished whole cultures and peoples. Even the experience of the UK, itself able to avoid occupation, was enough to make it acutely aware of its vulnerability in the age of the bomber and ballistic missile.

None of these four states face any plausible threat of large-scale invasion or annihilation today, and a similar situation applies to India. However, other states do still have such concerns. Pakistan, in particular, remains concerned that its continuing existence as a united, independent state has not been fully accepted by India. Its leaders recall India's role in the partition of their country in 1971, and the creation of the new state of Bangladesh as a consequence; and they fear that India could back secessionist movements within Pakistan, for example in Baluchistan, in pursuit of the country's dismemberment. In this insecure context, Pakistan's leaders view India's superiority in conventional forces with particular concern: in some circumstances, they believe it is possible that India would seek to use military force to pursue the destruction of Pakistan as a state. Pakistan's possession of nuclear weapons, it is believed, helps to deter such an invasion.

Unlike Pakistan, Russia faces no credible threat of extinction through military force; but its post-Cold War weakness in conventional forces has also driven it to put considerable emphasis on nuclear weapons in its defence doctrine. Neither NATO nor China has the capability (or desire) to seek to repeat Napoleon's and Hitler's failed efforts at total conquest of Russia. However, more limited conflicts on Russia's periphery, in which some in Russia might see a role for nuclear weapons, are certainly possible. During the Georgian conflict of 2008, for example, the fear of direct confrontation between US and Russian forces, with all the escalation possibilities this could have involved, persuaded President Bush to dismiss the idea of using limited US military options to stem the Russian advance.[16] Future political crises within Belarus, Ukraine or Central Asia could also provide opportunities for conflict. Given the massive US conventional air assets that could be deployed into the region at relatively short notice, the Russian government may believe that it may need a threat of nuclear escalation in order to prevent US intervention. The ease with which the US was able to overthrow regimes in Serbia, Afghanistan, Iraq and Libya, as well as NATO enlargement to former

---

[16] Ronald D Asmus, *A Little War that Shook the World: Georgia, Russia, and the Future of the West* (Basingstoke and New York: Palgrave Macmillan, 2009), as quoted in Gideon Rachman, 'Did Dick Cheney Want to Start a War with Russia?', *Financial Times*, 19 February 2010.

Soviet republics (the three Baltic republics and, potentially, Georgia and Ukraine), has deepened this fear.[17]

In order for either Pakistan or Russia to agree to complete nuclear abolition, these territorial insecurities would have to be addressed. Yet this does not mean that these two states could not be persuaded to accept the more limited objective of nuclear restraint at low numbers, providing that they believed that they could still retain an adequate capability for nuclear deterrence against potential invaders. This will not be easy; but it is (in present circumstances) largely specific to these two cases. The decline of conflict over territory since the Second World War, together with the decline of the large armies that provided invasion capabilities in the past, mean that none of the other acknowledged nuclear-armed states – the US, China, India, France and the UK – now experience a similar degree of territorial insecurity. Nor should the problem in the case of Russia be overstated. The sheer vastness of its territory, like that of China and India, provides a considerable safeguard against invasion and occupation, as does the progressive demobilisation of NATO's ground forces since the end of the Cold War.

Questionable Roles

The large arsenals of the US and Russia were built at a time when both believed that one or other state could achieve a meaningful nuclear 'superiority', either on the battlefield ('war-fighting') or through a disarming 'counterforce' first strike against an adversary's nuclear forces, with large numbers of nuclear weapons. These two operational roles are now considered in turn.

The Decline and Fall of Nuclear War-Fighting

In the earliest years of the nuclear age, large arsenals were associated with tactical war-fighting roles. Both the US and Soviet Union deployed thousands of weapons with their armies, air forces and navies, in order to shape potential battles to their advantage. Artillery units were equipped with short-range missiles and nuclear artillery shells. Surface ships were provided with nuclear-armed torpedoes, nuclear depth charges and anti-ship missiles, and submarines with cruise missiles. Air forces (based on land and at sea) were armed with nuclear free-fall bombs, air-to-air missiles and air-to-ground missiles.

In one incident at the height of the Cuban Missile Crisis, a US U-2 spy plane became lost and was detected as it mistakenly entered Soviet air space on 27 October 1962. Soviet aircraft were launched to intercept it and,

---

[17] Forrest E Morgan, 'Dancing with the Bear: Managing Escalation in a Conflict with Russia', *IFRI Proliferation Papers* (No. 40, Winter 2012), pp. 37–39.

in reply, US F-102 interceptors were scrambled from their air base in western Alaska. Their only means of defence was a nuclear-armed Falcon air-to-air missile, which the pilot had the physical ability to launch by himself. Had these aircraft met their Soviet opposite numbers, the first act of a third world war could have been a US fighter pilot shooting down multiple Soviet aircraft with a nuclear weapon.[18]

As US and Soviet planners on both sides began to understand better how tactical nuclear weapons could be used, they increasingly came to the view that they were of little operational value in a military conflict on the ground. Very high levels of damage could be caused, leading to large numbers of casualties and the rendering of vast areas, even whole countries, uninhabitable. Yet NATO scenario-planning suggested that, in the event that the Soviet Union was thought to be on the verge of overcoming NATO's conventional defences with its own conventional forces, first use of tactical nuclear weapons by NATO, followed by a similar Soviet response, would not have altered the final outcome.[19]

A similar pattern of analysis and thinking, it is now clear, was developing within the Soviet military by the 1970s:[20]

[T]he Soviet military command understood the consequences of nuclear war and was intent on preventing it. The General Staff, beginning in the 1970s, developed the idea that nuclear weapons were a political tool, with very limited military utility . . . [They] did not prepare any detailed plans for extended combat on a nuclear battlefield . . . Although the Soviets developed limited nuclear options, they neither discussed nor exercised initiating selective nuclear use . . . Soviet military leaders also were very skeptical about the escalation control and expected the period of limited nuclear exchanges in theater to last at most for several days.

Some have suggested that there may be specific naval-related scenarios – such as opposing amphibious landings or attacking carrier task forces – in which a tactical use of nuclear weapons could be of operational value in an asymmetric conflict.[21] This helps to explain the particular attachment of the

---

[18] Michael Dobbs, *One Minute to Midnight: Kennedy, Khrushchev and Castro on the Brink of Nuclear War* (New York: Vintage Books, 2009), pp. 254–75.
[19] Interviews with former UK officials, 2011.
[20] John G Hines, Ellis Mishulovich and John F Shull, *Soviet Intentions 1965–1985. Vol. I: An Analytical Comparison of U.S-Soviet Assessments During the Cold War* (McLean, VA: The BDM Corporation, 22 September, 1995), p. 44, cited in John A Battilega, 'Soviet Views of Nuclear Warfare', in Henry D Sokolski (ed.), *Getting MAD: Nuclear Mutual Assured Destruction, Its Origins and Practice* (Carlisle, PA: Strategic Studies Institute, 2004).
[21] See, for example, Soviet discussion of using nuclear weapons to oppose a US invasion of Cuba in Aleksandr Fursenko and Timothy Naftali, *One Hell of a Gamble: Khrushchev, Castro and Kennedy, 1958–1964* (New York: W W Norton, 1997), pp. 240–43.

Russian Navy to tactical nuclear weapons, which it continues to justify as a necessary balance to the greatly superior conventional capabilities of US maritime forces.

It is less clear, however, whether Russia's wider reliance on tactical nuclear weapons outside the maritime context is increasing or decreasing. Declaratory policy – as reflected in political speeches and published doctrine – continues to emphasise the central role of nuclear weapons in Russian defence thinking; but almost all the considerable investments now being planned for new nuclear systems relate to the country's strategic forces. By contrast, as a recent study by Igor Sutyagin points out, the number of operational NSNW systems has fallen sharply over the last two decades, paralleling the sharp decline in the size of the conventional forces that provide the platforms on which these weapons can be deployed. Out of a total deployed NSNW arsenal of around 1,000 warheads, 300 are naval and up to a further 200 are air-defence warheads, likely to be phased out shortly. This could leave a total of only 500 or so NSNW with Russia's air and ground forces, compared with the 150–200 US weapons deployed in Europe.[22] If these estimates are correct, they could suggest that Russia's armed forces, like their Soviet predecessors in the 1970s and 1980s, are sceptical of the need for a massive NSNW arsenal as a war-fighting substitute for ground-based conventional forces.

Warning Shots
The withdrawal of both the US and Russia from a nuclear war-fighting role (at least on land) does not mean that the two countries have ruled out other roles for non-strategic nuclear weapons. Russia has made clear that it wants to maintain the ability to use NSNW in order to signal, if necessary, its willingness to escalate to strategic nuclear use if an opponent is not willing to desist from, or limit, its aggression. In serving this 'de-escalation' mission, Russia's NSNW arguably perform a role not dissimilar to that performed by the remaining NATO nuclear-capable aircraft deployed in Europe. Importantly, in both NATO and Russia, the numerical requirements for such a role are much less demanding than the more open-ended requirements for war-fighting. In the short and medium term, the numbers of NSNW deployed by both the US and Russia will continue to be shaped by bureaucratic momentum and (in the case of the US) alliance politics. Over time, however, the lack of a credible operational requirement for a large NSNW force may make it easier for both countries to reduce their arsenals.

There continues to be a debate as to just how few NSNW is enough for the US. Some will argue that the warning-shot role could be performed

---

[22] Igor Sutyagin, 'Russian Non-Strategic Nuclear Potential: Developing a New Estimate', RUSI Occasional Paper (forthcoming, 2012).

by US strategic bombers armed with stand-off cruise missiles. Others will argue that the US still needs the B-61 gravity bomb, based on both strategic bombers and Europe-deployed F-35 aircraft, for this purpose.[23] Even if a separate non-strategic system is thought to be needed, however, only a small number of warheads may be required solely for this signalling role.

Further evidence of the compatibility between a 'warning-shot' requirement and small force size is provided by the nuclear doctrines of the UK and France. The concept also formed a key part of early Israeli discussion of circumstances in which it might use its nuclear force, with Cohen reporting 'a consensus (in the late 1960s) that Israel's first nuclear detonation had to be a *demonstration* for deterrence purposes'.[24] It was also a core part of South Africa's 'catalytic' posture in the 1980s, when it believed that a threat to use its small arsenal could help deter Soviet aggression by inducing intervention by friendly outside powers in the event of a regional conflict. Indeed, in this case, a demonstration capability substituted altogether for a strategic role.[25]

One of the worrying features of Pakistan's nuclear programme, by contrast, is that it is widely believed to be is seeking to develop both a demonstration and war-fighting capability. Its acquisition of the 60 km-range Hatf-9 (Nasr) missiles is widely seen in this light. For, whereas forces designed to provide warning-shot capabilities can be deployed some distance from a potential battlefield, short-range weapons designed for tactical roles must be capable of being deployed forwards in times of crisis. As in the Cold War, the threat of such deployment may make a potential opponent fear inadvertent escalation as a result of unauthorised use by battlefield commanders.[26] However, it may also increase incentives for pre-emptive attack at an early stage of a crisis, especially if this could prevent dispersal of these weapons into the field. In contrast to the warning-shot requirement, moreover, Pakistan's apparent desire for a war-fighting capability could generate a more open-ended requirement for an ever-larger tactical arsenal, with each Indian advance (actual or potential) in pre-emptive or defensive conventional capabilities leading to further Pakistani demands for tactical nuclear weapons.

---

[23] For a useful summary of the areas of disagreement on this, see James M Acton and Elbridge Colby, 'Nuclear Weapons – Something We Can All Agree On', *thehill.com*, 24 May 2012.

[24] Avner Cohen, *The Worst-Kept Secret: Israel's Bargain with the Bomb* (New York: Columbia University Press, 2011), p. 78.

[25] Peter Liberman, 'The Rise and Fall of the South African Bomb', *International Security* (Vol. 26, No. 2, Fall 2001), pp. 45–86.

[26] Feroz Hassan Khan, 'Minimum Deterrence: Pakistan's Dilemma', in Malcolm Chalmers, Andrew Somerville and Andrea Berger (eds.), 'Small Nuclear Forces: Five Perspectives', RUSI Whitehall Report, 3–11, December 2011, p. 73.

Disarming Counterforce

The large arsenals of the Cold War superpowers, however, were also developed to meet a second operational rationale: the minimisation of damage (a difficult objective to achieve in a nuclear age) through building a capability for pre-emptive strikes against the nuclear forces of an opposing force. This in turn meant having a force that was capable of promptly destroying a very high proportion of enemy strategic nuclear forces before they could be launched. Such a force, clearly, was of little value in retaliation for a large-scale enemy first strike, when enemy missile silos and bomber bases would be empty. Its main operational value, therefore, had to be as a means of limiting the damage that an opponent could cause in response. Such a capability, it should be emphasised, was not seen by US leaders as one that would be used 'out of the blue' in peacetime. Rather, it was argued, the capability for such action would deter the Soviet Union from using conventional forces or tactical nuclear weapons in a way that might risk escalation to a strategic nuclear exchange.

The availability of large stockpiles (and the need to provide a rationale for their existence) may have been driving doctrine more than doctrine was driving capabilities. As numbers of warheads grew, political leaders were encouraged to ask for higher levels of assurance that targets would be destroyed. High levels of secrecy, together with lack of political involvement in the details of nuclear war-planning, contributed to this inflation of weapon requirements.[27]

If stable nuclear restraint is to be achieved at low numbers, it would have to be constructed in such a way that it could not be seen as making a disarming first strike by the US (or any other state) on another nuclear-armed state more feasible than it currently is.

Provided that the adversary in question is capable of deploying a range of readily available counter-measures, the requirements for this condition to be met should not be overstated. However, concerns over possible disarming first strikes by an adversary may mean that 'minimum' nuclear forces will have to be significantly higher than would otherwise be necessary. As a result, proposals for mutual restraint positing a reduction in national arsenals to only tens of warheads per country (rather than hundreds) could be seen to be encouraging pre-emption in a crisis, thus, paradoxically, making nuclear war more likely. For it is the prospect that weapons could be detonated in one's own cities that is the critical element in 'unacceptable damage', not the total number of weapons that a potential adversary possesses.

---

[27] For an insider's perspective of the interaction between force size and targeting requirements, see Jerry Miller, *Stockpile: The Story Behind 10,000 Strategic Nuclear Weapons* (Annapolis, MD: Naval Institute Press, 2010).

However, a minimum-deterrent posture would mean that the US and Russia would have to forego a credible capability for a disarming first strike against a nuclear-armed adversary, instead accepting a state of mutual vulnerability or 'mutually assured destruction'. This is nothing new between the US and Russia, and has long been accepted as a reality amongst the political elites of both countries. It will be harder for the US to accept in relation to China, with domestic 'hawks' still wanting to press ahead with developments (including conventional strike and missile defence) that give some hope that mutual deterrence is not inevitable. Given China's emergence as a second superpower, such an argument may fade over time, as it did in relation to the Soviet Union in the early 1960s. The more that the US resists accepting mutual vulnerability in relation to China, however, the greater the risk that this will encourage China to build its own offensive capabilities, for example by adding multiple warheads to its ballistic missiles. The result – mutual vulnerability – would be the same, but at significantly higher numbers.

Mutual acceptance of vulnerability is also a condition for some degree of stability in both the Pakistan-India and India-China nuclear relationships. Both India (in the former case) and China (in the latter case) may chafe against this reality and seek means to blunt it through defensive counter-measures. As in the US-Russia relationship, however, the main effect of such measures (if successful) would be to drive the number of weapons in offensive arsenals upwards.

The US should, in principle, find it relatively easier to reduce its nuclear force to low numbers if both Russia and China are willing to accept comparable restraint in their own nuclear forces. Its unquestioned position as the world's leading maritime power means that its missile submarines (which host most of its strategic warheads) are likely to remain invulnerable to attack for the foreseeable future. No other state has any realistic prospect of being able to launch a successful pre-emptive strike (nuclear or conventional) on its bomber forces, given their ability to disperse widely during a crisis. Furthermore, no other state has deployed missile defences that could significantly degrade a large-scale attack on its territory. The US could therefore reduce its nuclear force to 300 warheads or fewer and still maintain the ability to inflict levels of damage on an adversary in a retaliatory strike that would be out of all proportion to any possible political gain that it might be seeking.

Indeed, even if the US had only one (out of fourteen) Ohio-class submarines available, it would have the ability to launch ninety-six W-76 warheads, each with an estimated yield of 100 kilotons, against an adversary. The detonation of most of these weapons on the territory of Russia, or China or any other state would be a disaster beyond measure for that country. The credibility of such a deterrent would not rely, therefore, on the US's technical capability, but on whether others would ever believe that US leaders would find any political cause that justified a decision to inflict destruction on such an unprecedented scale, except in retaliation against a nuclear attack. Yet, as the world's only military superpower, with a margin of superiority in conventional military force over any potential rival that has never before been experienced, the US has a particular interest in limiting the role of nuclear weapons in international security to the deterrence of nuclear use by others. Even if it remains unwilling to declare a formal policy of 'sole purpose' or 'No First Use', the scenarios in which the US would find it to be in its interests to threaten first use remain far-fetched and improbable.

By the late 2020s or 2030s, it is possible to imagine scenarios in which China gains conventional superiority over the US in the western Pacific, raising the possibility that the US might be convinced that it would lose a battle for control of the Taiwan Straits or the Sea of Japan. Even in such a world, however, the risks that China would incur were it to attack US forward-based forces would be massive. For some considerable time to come, the US will still have global forces that could be surged into the region in order to reverse any Chinese gains, and at a pace that would likely be much more rapid than in the 1940s. As long as it clearly has such options, it is difficult to see why US threats of nuclear first use could be seen as either necessary or proportionate.

Extended Deterrence and the Conventional Balance
Some analysts believe that the credibility of extended nuclear deterrence depends on the US having the ability to threaten a disarming first strike on the nuclear forces of a potential adversary. With such a capability, it is argued, a potential adversary would not be able to deter the US from intervention in support of its allies by threatening escalation to a nuclear exchange that could put the US homeland at risk. Rather, provided that the US had a meaningful first-strike capability, the adversary would be deterred from aggressive action by the knowledge that, if necessary, the US could prevail in a nuclear exchange. Thus, for example, Keir A Lieber and Daryl G Press argue that: 'Unless the United States maintains potent counterforce capabilities, U.S. adversaries may conclude – perhaps correctly – that the United States' strategic position abroad rests largely on a bluff.'[28]

---

[28] Keir A Lieber and Daryl G Press, 'The Nukes We Need: Preserving the American Deterrent', *Foreign Affairs* (November/December 2009). See also the discussion of this paper by Jan Lodal, James M Acton, Hans M Kristensen, Matthew McKinzie and Ivan Oelrich, 'Second Strike: Is the US Nuclear Arsenal Outmoded', *Foreign Affairs* (March/April 2010).

The US has historically set great store on the advantages that it can obtain by exploiting technological advantage for military gain. However, as in the past, there are limits as to how far this process can be taken, especially when facing innovative and determined adversaries.

These limits are especially evident in relation to the US's nuclear relations with Russia and China, both of which continue to invest in a wide range of counter-measures against a possible US counterforce attack. Efforts to maintain and strengthen first-strike nuclear capabilities against Russia and China are therefore likely to be both unrealistic and potentially counterproductive. Both countries are already investing in new warheads, missiles and satellites, new anti-BMD and anti-satellite systems, offensive cyber-sabotage capabilities, enhanced concealment and protection measures, counter-surveillance capabilities, and many other means designed to thwart a US offensive. Given these counter-measures, the US cannot be confident that it will ever have useable nuclear superiority – that is, the ability to prevent any significant nuclear retaliation – against either Russia or China.

Changes in regional conventional balances, however, could throw up difficult issues for the US's relations with its European and Asian allies that cannot be resolved through more robust nuclear guarantees. During the Cold War, the US's willingness to extend nuclear security guarantees to key allies in Europe and East Asia played an important role in heading off further proliferation in these two regions; but it also led to concerns over the credibility of those guarantees, particularly where a potential opponent had developed the capability to reach the continental US with nuclear weapons.

Given the extent of US post-Cold War conventional superiority, such concerns now focus on whether the US would be willing to respond promptly with conventional forces in a crisis involving a nuclear-armed power (such as Russia or China). Given the experience of Georgia in 2008, for example, would Russia believe that the US would intervene to reverse an incursion into Estonia? Or would China believe that the US was willing to back up its security guarantee to Japan with military force if China were to attempt forcefully to assert its claim to disputed waters in the East China Sea (or the Sea of Japan)?

The answer to such questions does not lie, however, in the size or deployment of the US's nuclear weapons, the use of which would be entirely disproportionate (and therefore incredible) in such scenarios. Rather, it would depend on whether the US was seen to be willing to respond promptly and unconditionally with conventional forces, and this is where the bulk of US reassurance efforts are rightly directed. Paradoxically, therefore, the stronger alternative conventional options are, the weaker the credibility of any implied threats of nuclear first use that might be made.

The role of nuclear weapons in US extended deterrence, by contrast, is most credible in circumstances that are less likely but more serious – such as large-scale invasion of, or nuclear attack on, Japan. As with conventional forces, the credibility of US commitment in such circumstances would result more from politics than from numbers. Extended deterrence considerations could make the US more reluctant to accept a large margin of numerical inferiority in nuclear forces *vis-à-vis* Russia or China, out of concern that this could be misinterpreted by its more exposed allies. Yet it would not be a reason for the US to oppose mutual restraint at low numbers, provided that Russia and China make similar commitments.

US Hegemony and Nuclear Restraint

An important argument against further nuclear restraint comes from those in the US who argue that deep nuclear cuts, even if undertaken by the US and Russia in concert, would trade in an advantage which the US has worked hard to accrue over many years, while asking little from the smaller nuclear-armed states in return.

The advantages of complete nuclear abolition for the US are clear, removing one of the few capabilities that weaker opponents can use to deter outside military intervention, and thus allowing the US to take fuller advantage of its position as the world's most capable conventional military power. Many of the arguments made for the US to adopt a policy of No First Use make the same point, suggesting that the US's advantages in conventional forces give it a particular interest in such a policy. For example, Gerson argues that:[29]

> Since the end of the Cold [War], the United States is the dominant conventional power. The United States rightly places great importance on maintaining conventional superiority and global power projection, and despite the ongoing development of anti-access and area-denial capabilities – especially China's development of an anti-ship ballistic missile – U.S. conventional military capabilities and defense spending vastly outstrip those of every other nation. Consequently, the threat of nuclear first use is unnecessary to deter conventional aggression, and, if deterrence fails, unnecessary to help win the conflict because there is no country that can defeat the United States in a major conventional war.

This argument would apply, with added force, in the event of complete nuclear disarmament, which is one of the reasons why some conventionally weaker nuclear-armed states (though not China) are sceptical about the prospect.

If abolition is not achievable, however, some in the US may wonder why it should be prepared to give up the advantages that its large arsenal

---

[29] Michael S Gerson, 'No First Use: The Next Step for US Nuclear Policy', *International Security* (Vol. 35, No. 2, Fall 2010), p. 18.

provides. Such concerns take a variety of forms. As already discussed, some argue that the US's unique responsibilities as a provider of nuclear extended deterrence require it to maintain a larger nuclear arsenal than states concerned only with national defence. Others contend that the US should only be prepared to accept reductions in its nuclear arsenal provided that it continues to improve its strategic missile defence capabilities, with a view to providing an effective counter to China's – and perhaps, in time, even Russia's – offensive forces.

Scientific and industrial stakeholders also have an interest in maintaining a large and diverse arsenal, and provide a strong counterpoint to those (including successive presidents, both Republican and Democrat) who have sought to make further nuclear arms reductions. The strength of these countervailing pressures was seen in the vigorous opposition to the relatively modest cuts in strategic nuclear forces agreed in the New START Treaty with Russia. While the treaty was eventually ratified with seventy-one votes in favour in the US Senate (four more than were required), the administration had to agree large increases in the budgets of the nuclear laboratories in order to achieve this result. The decline in traditions of foreign-policy bipartisanship has further increased the difficulties involved in making substantial policy changes, thus creating a 'status quo bias' in nuclear policy, and indeed, arguably, more widely.

These difficulties may shed some light on how hard it could be for the world's only military superpower to give up capabilities that are a result of unprecedented investments over many years. One recent estimate suggests that the US spent $8.7 trillion (in 2010 prices) on nuclear forces between 1940 and 2010. This accounted for a massive 29 per cent of all defence expenditure (and almost 11 per cent of all federal government spending) during the period up to 1996, reflecting the heavy emphasis placed on nuclear weapons in US security policy during this period.[30] The US's total nuclear stockpile has fallen from 22,217 in 1989 to 5,113 in 2009, with commensurate reductions in both 'strategic' and 'non-strategic' delivery systems.[31] Even so, US annual spending on nuclear forces and related capabilities (including missile defence) in 2008 was still estimated

---

[30] Stephen I Schwartz, 'Unaccountable: Exploring the Lack of Budgetary Transparency for U.S. Nuclear Security Spending', Nuclear Threat Initiative, 5 January 2012, <http://www.nti.org/analysis/articles/transparency-us-nuclear-security-budget/>, accessed 8 August 2012.
[31] US Department of Defense, 'Fact Sheet: Increasing Transparency in the U.S. Nuclear Weapons Stockpile, May 2010', <http://www.defense.gov/npr/docs/10-05-03_Fact_Sheet_US_Nuclear_Transparency_FINAL_w_Date.pdf>, accessed 8 August 2012.

to have been at least $52 billion.[32] While this accounted for only 7 per cent of the US's total defence budget, it was almost as much as other major powers (such as France, Russia and the UK) each spent on defence in total.[33]

The level of resources devoted to this effort helps to explain the reluctance of many of those most associated with nuclear weapons policy to embrace proposals for deep cuts. Having invested so much for so long (both financially and personally) in the nuclear enterprise, they view proposals for radical downsizing as a betrayal of that investment. While such concerns could, in principle, be assuaged by radical changes in the international environmental, these 'sunk costs' do make it more difficult politically to embrace the radical change that deep cuts in nuclear forces would involve. Within the next decade or so, further reductions in strategic force levels will probably be needed in order to defer large new investments in replacement delivery systems (notably new missile submarines); but these pressures will not begin to have much significant impact until the latter part of this decade, building steadily thereafter. Moreover, even without new spending on replacement delivery systems, the US could probably maintain a strategic nuclear force of well over 1,000 deployed warheads until well into the 2020s.

This tendency towards nuclear conservatism, generated in part by a reluctance to give up expensively procured systems, is reinforced by a wider geopolitical narrative. For example, Robert Kagan argued in February 2012 that:[34]

> There is little reason to believe that a return to multipolarity in the 21st century would bring greater peace and stability than in the past. The era of American predominance has shown that there is no better recipe for great-power peace than certainty about who holds the upper hand.

Those US policy-makers with this worldview may be instinctively more reluctant to surrender strategic capabilities that are still a potent symbol of US superiority, and may instead want the US to continue to set the technological pace in strategic competition, forcing others (including

---

[32] Stephen I Schwartz with Deepti Choubey, 'Nuclear Security Spending: Assessing Costs, Examining Priorities', Carnegie Endowment for International Peace, January 2009, p. 6.

[33] A more recent study has estimated total spending on 'strategic nuclear offensive forces' in 2011 at $33 billion. This excludes other costs related to the 'broader nuclear enterprise', such as spending on missile defence, tactical nuclear weapons and environmental clean-up of former nuclear sites. See Russell Rumbaugh and Nathan Cohn, *Resolving Ambiguity: Costing Nuclear Weapons* (Washington, DC: The Henry L Stimson Center, June 2012).

[34] Robert Kagan, 'Why the World Needs America', *Wall Street Journal*, 11 February 2012.

Russia and China) to be concerned about what the US might do next. They will be more reluctant to acquiesce to the symbolic acceptance of mutual vulnerability to nuclear attack than are other major powers – including China – with more modest aspirations and capabilities. They may also be more inclined to believe that technological prowess (as evident, for example, in high hopes for what future missile defences can achieve) can allow the US to exempt itself from the dependence on others that this vulnerability creates.

Mutual nuclear restraint at low numbers, by contrast, may feel more comfortable for those who believe that it is possible to use international co-operative regimes to pursue US interests, as successive US administrations have done since the Second World War. In particular, the pursuit of nuclear restraint at low numbers is consistent with a policy of widening the scope of effective multilateralism to incorporate states – such as Russia, China, India and Brazil – that were not part of post-war Western institutions, but are increasingly important actors as a result of their rapid economic development. It could also help meet the US's broader objective of deepening mutual security confidence-building with Russia and China. In order to do so, however, it will need to be willing to go some way to address the concerns that both countries still have in relation to future US strategic capabilities, for example in relation to missile defence and conventional strike.

Meeting these specific concerns on mutual nuclear vulnerability, however, would not mean that the US needs to give up its wider advantages in military force. The US's margin of advantage in conventional military power has grown, quantitatively and qualitatively, over the last three decades, and shows no sign of eroding significantly for at least another decade. It is greatly strengthened, moreover, by its military alliances with strong and capable states in Europe and Asia. It is possible to imagine scenarios in which the US would lack immediate conventional superiority in the event of a surprise enemy offensive in a particular location, and as a result might take some time to amass the forces necessary to restore the *status quo ante*. Nevertheless, all other states, including China and Russia, remain acutely aware that they will continue to have to shape their own security policies under the shadow of wider US conventional superiority. This wider context in turn greatly limits the ability of other states to use nuclear forces for purposes other than the 'fundamental roles' of deterrence against nuclear attack and invasion. Moving towards nuclear restraint at low numbers will make little difference to this picture.

Yet the US's position as the single global superpower also makes it more difficult – certainly compared with the UK, France or even China – for it to accept the symbolism of having a nuclear force that is markedly smaller than those of other major powers. It probably does not matter in operational terms whether the US has rather fewer deployed weapons than Russia or China, especially since its own forces are generally much less vulnerable to attack. However, political optics, reinforced by decades of US-Russia arms control organised around the principle of parity, dictate that relative numbers do matter, both in the US and for others' perceptions of US power. For the foreseeable future, therefore, the US is likely to insist that its nuclear arsenal should not be seen to be noticeably smaller than that of any other state. The meaning of such a commitment is open to various interpretations, depending on whether, for example, one includes only strategic and operational weapons in the count. Yet, as the 2010 Nuclear Posture Review acknowledges, it imposes real constraints on US policy-makers:[35]

> Russia's nuclear force will remain a significant factor in determining how much and how fast we are prepared to reduce U.S. forces. Because of our improved relations, the need for strict numerical parity between the two countries is no longer as compelling as it was during the Cold War. But large disparities in nuclear capabilities could raise concerns on both sides and among U.S. allies and partners, and may not be conducive to maintaining a stable, long-term strategic relationship, especially as nuclear forces are significantly reduced. Therefore, we will place importance on Russia joining us as we move to lower levels.

This American political reality means that, whatever the technical arguments as to whether and how the US could safely move to adopt a nuclear posture more similar to that of the smaller nuclear-armed states, the US's room for movement in this regard is likely to be constrained by whether Russia is prepared to move in the same direction.

Russia is Indispensable

The Soviet Union and the US were in many respects nuclear twins, albeit not identical ones. They were the first countries to develop nuclear and thermonuclear weapons, followed by intercontinental bombers and missiles. Within two decades of Hiroshima, both had built arsenals numbering in the tens of thousands. Military postures were developed that provided nuclear weapons with a wide range of roles, stretching from tactical employment (depth charges, air-to-air missiles, land mines, artillery and so on) to strategic counterforce. Both devoted a large part of their defence budgets, which were in turn an order of magnitude bigger than those of any other power, to their nuclear forces. Their nuclear forces were seen not only as a reflection of their joint status as the only two

---

[35] US Department of Defense, 'Nuclear Posture Review Report 2010', p. 30.

superpowers, but also as their primary instrument for deterrence and, if necessary, military confrontation.

Since the end of the Cold War, however, the size of the Russian nuclear force has been sharply reduced, from an estimated 37,000 in 1990 to around 10,000 as of early 2012.[36] Only 4,400 warheads out of the total in 2012 are estimated to be assigned to the armed forces, with the remaining 5,500 retired and awaiting dismantlement.

As in the US, however, the pace at which the size of the Russian nuclear force has declined has been slowed by political factors. First, industrial and military constituencies related to the nuclear and missile programmes have remained significant in shaping security and procurement policy, acting as a constraint on more rapid reductions. Many thousands of workers, and large and lucrative procurement contracts, are tied up in the design, development and production of new missiles and submarines. Secondly, Russia's leadership has continued to see the maintenance of numerical parity with the US (and superiority compared with China and others) as an important reflection of its international status. Formal US recognition of this status, through SALT 1, was viewed by Soviet leaders at the time as being important, not least because it politically legitimised a state that US leaders had hitherto often described in terms akin to those used for 'rogue states' today. Russian leaders no longer believe it is possible to achieve equal status to the US in overall power; but they may be instinctively reluctant to give up one of the few indicators of such status that remain.

In Russia's case, moreover, these political drivers for maintaining high numbers are reinforced by security concerns. The two decades after the Cold War were characterised by a marked reduction in Russian relative conventional power, as it stood by helplessly as the US led bombing campaigns against erstwhile allies, including Serbia and Iraq. The borders of NATO were extended to within 100 miles of Russia's second city, St Petersburg, as a result of the entry of the three Baltic republics into the Alliance. The US made clear that it supported NATO membership for Ukraine and Georgia, and 'colour revolutions' in both countries were seen as part of a wider Western effort to undermine Russia's remaining ex-Soviet sphere of influence. US transit arrangements in Central Asia, necessary for its operations in Afghanistan and negotiated with the acquiescence of Russia, were also seen in this light.

Yet, in part as a result of the economic crisis that engulfed Russia after 1991, its conventional military capabilities are now a pale shadow of those

---

[36] Robert S Norris and Hans M Kristensen, 'Global Nuclear Weapons Inventories, 1945–2010', *Bulletin of the Atomic Scientists* (Vol. 66, No. 4, July/August 2010), p. 78; Hans M Kristensen and Robert S Norris, 'Russian Nuclear Forces, 2012', *Bulletin of the Atomic Scientists* (Vol. 68, No. 2, March/April 2012), p. 88.

the Soviet Union possessed in the 1980s. This decline, combined with the US's demonstrably effective conventional capabilities, has magnified concerns over Russia's military vulnerability. This has made Russia more reluctant than the US to reduce the tactical roles that it assigned to nuclear weapons (for example, their role in combating US carrier battlegroups deploying near Russian missile submarine sanctuaries). It has also deepened pre-existing concerns over US capabilities for combined air strikes against Russia itself. Ever since the 1980s, Soviet and then Russian leaders have feared that the US could use its technological edge to overwhelm Russia's large, but relatively poor quality, conventional defences. US plans for national missile defence are viewed as part of this wider trend, to which Russia will need to respond if it is not to open itself up to political domination by the US.

Such a line of reasoning may seem far-fetched and even absurd to American and European ears, and indeed to many within Russia itself. After all, with both European and now American defence budgets falling and many other more urgent military challenges elsewhere, the last thing on NATO minds is attacking Russia. However, in Russia, as in other major powers, the memory of the Second World War continues to frame security thinking both consciously and even subconsciously, as does the more recent experience of the Cold War.

This conservative approach to defence planning has been further reinforced by the imperatives of domestic politics, most recently demonstrated in Vladimir Putin's successful campaign for re-election as Russia's president. In his campaign, Putin promised to spend 23 trillion roubles ($770 billion) over the next decade on military modernisation, and to press ahead with new generations of ICBMs (intercontinental ballistic missiles) and ballistic missile submarines.[37]

It is questionable, however, whether the Russian state has the resources needed to finance these ambitious plans, given both its heavy reliance on hydrocarbon revenues and the competing demands of the many other constituencies to whom Putin has also made electoral pledges. Given the inefficiency and corruption of its military-industrial complex, moreover, it is far from clear whether extra spending, on its own, will allow Russia to narrow the technological gap that has opened up between itself and the US.[38]

As of 2011, Russia was estimated to be spending $72 billion annually on defence, almost 4 per cent of its GDP and the world's third-largest military budget. Yet this total was not much more than the $60 billion spent by the UK in the same year, and amounted to only one-tenth of the $710 billion spent by the US. Even if the spending gap with the US narrows

---

[37] Dmitri Trenin, 'Putin's National Security Vision', Carnegie Endowment Commentary, 23 February 2012.

[38] Stockholm International Peace Research Institute, '17 April 2012: World Military Spending Levels Out after 13 Years of Increases, Says SIPRI', 17 April 2012.

somewhat in the next decade as a result of the latter's austerity drive, it will still leave Russia in a position of being essentially a medium power, not a superpower, in terms of overall military capabilities. Its dilemmas are likely to be increased further by continuing growth in China's defence effort, currently consuming around $143 billion annually but due to rise rapidly over the next decade.[39] The fundamental driver for this inequality, *vis-à-vis* both the US and China, lies in Russia's relative economic and demographic position, which means it is strongly in Russia's security interests not to be drawn into a new arms race with either of these two economic giants.

'Objectively speaking', as Russians are fond of saying, it should be in the country's interests to seek to demilitarise its relations with its powerful neighbours to the west and east. Yet such an approach has little support within the current government, which argues that appeasement of the West in the immediate post-Cold War period led only to an intensification of the country's encirclement (seen, for example, in NATO enlargement) and economic crisis. Since President Putin came to power in 1999, therefore, an important plank of his domestic appeal has been his commitment to restore Russia's position as a significant military power, prepared to act robustly to defend its interests. Even as Russia has continued to reduce the size of its nuclear arsenal, therefore, it has maintained a strong emphasis on the role of nuclear weapons in defending the country from external (and especially US) aggression.

Parity for All?
While maintenance of the principle of broad numerical parity will be important to maintain support for further reductions in both the US and Russia, however, it cannot be the basis for mutual restraint once other states are brought into the process. Rising powers like China and India are unlikely to be willing to accept permanent ceilings on their nuclear forces lower than those for the US or Russia, even if they have no intention of building up to their level. Even the UK, which has now reduced its nuclear arsenal to a level well below that of France, may be reluctant to institutionalise this inequality in a legally binding agreement.[40]

Further complexity would be added because of the need to take alliances, including hypothetical future alliances, into account in a world of

---

[39] *Ibid.*
[40] James Acton argues that rejection by the UK, France or China of 'a treaty that formally enshrines inequality' would make it 'extremely unlikely' for Russia and the United States to continue reductions. James M Acton, 'Low Numbers: A Practical Path to Deep Reductions', Carnegie Endowment for International Peace, March 2011, p. 56. His point reinforces this paper's contention that alternatives to a formal binding limit would have to be found if mutual restraint at low numbers were to be made possible.

unequal arms-control ceilings. If the balance of nuclear numbers matters, it will be argued, Russia will have a legitimate concern if it is outnumbered by the three NATO Nuclear-Weapon States combined, a concern that will be heightened if the Big Two reduce their arsenals to a level near to those of the Small Three. India, for its part, could complain about the possibility that Pakistan might take advantage of an India-China conflict to seek gains of its own.[41] The US could worry about a Russia-India-China alliance reviving an alignment from the 1950s. China, which could have the world's largest economy by 2025, might look at the balance between its own forces and those of the 'encircling alliance' that might be arraigned against it by the US, India and Russia, not to speak of the intercontinental missiles of the UK and France.

If mutual restraint between the nuclear-armed states is to be successful, therefore, it would need to reject the notion that the relative sizes of nuclear forces bear any relation to deterrent capability or to political prestige. The US, in addition, would need to be convinced that its ability to provide deterrence assurances to its allies did not depend on maintaining numerical nuclear superiority over potential adversaries.

This does not mean that the size of national arsenals is no longer related to deterrence capability. Each state would still be able to maintain a nuclear force capable of inflicting unacceptable levels of damage on a potential adversary, even after allowing for attrition as a result of enemy pre-emption or defences. Insofar as the nuclear forces of one state could play a direct role in such pre-emption, moreover, their capabilities would continue to shape those of its potential opponent. Such a calculation, however, would privilege a requirement for stability through mutual vulnerability rather than a requirement for strict numerical parity.

An important element in nuclear restraint at low numbers, therefore, could be for the Big Two to adopt nuclear postures much more similar to those of France, the UK and China. A recent example of a proposal consistent with this model came from a group of US Air Force analysts in 2010, who argued that:[42]

> America's nuclear security can rest easily on a relatively small number of counterforce and countervalue weapons totalling just over 300. Moreover, it does not matter if Russia, who is America's biggest competitor in this arena, follows suit. The relative advantage the Russians might gain in theory does not exist in reality. Even if one were

---

[41] James M Acton, *Deterrence During Disarmament: Deep Nuclear Reductions and International Security*, Adelphi Paper 417 (Abingdon: Routledge for IISS, 2011), p. 88.
[42] James Wood Forsyth Jr, B Chance Saltzman, Gary Schaub Jr, 'Remembrance of Things Past: The Enduring Value of Nuclear Weapons', *Strategic Studies Quarterly* (Spring 2010), pp. 74–89.

to assume the worst – a bolt from the blue that took out all of America's ICBMs – the Russians would leave their cities at risk and therefore remain deterred from undertaking the first move . . .

[T]he United States is deterred in most contingencies by China, which has a much smaller force structure. Presumably, if China can deter the United States, small numbers are effective. In fact, arguments for a large force have no meaning unless they are tied to an exclusive counterforce strategy directed against Russia, which, when all is said and done, does not appear to be necessary. During the Cold War, the superpowers raced to increase numbers in an attempt to prevent one side from acquiring either a counterforce capability or a symbolic numerical advantage. All the while, both sides lost sight of the fact that it is the political value of nuclear weapons that matters most, not their military utility. New nuclear states seem satisfied with small numbers. One wonders why.

Cutting their force to levels comparable to those of the Small Three would mean the US and Russia giving up current capabilities for the destruction of the entire nuclear and military infrastructure of the other; nevertheless, the Big Two would still retain an assured retaliatory capability that could cause a level of damage greater than any of the states concerned suffered in the Second World War, but within days rather than over a period of years. A capability for destroying as few as ten or twenty separate targets in an adversary's territory would be sufficient for this purpose. Even once allowance had been made for unavailability and attrition through various causes, such a destructive capability should not require a total stockpile that is numbered in more than the low hundreds.

For the reasons already discussed, large arsenals of tactical nuclear weapons would also be redundant. It would take many years before reserve warhead stocks, amounting to several thousand on each side, could be fully dismantled; but reductions in operationally deployed arsenals, from around 2,000 at present to around 300 (the current size of French and Chinese forces), could be completed rather quickly once the decision to do so had been taken.

There would be a question (especially, perhaps, for China) as to whether such reductions should be conditional on a parallel process for India and Pakistan. The key issue of wider concern in relation to these two states, however, may not be the precise number of warheads they possess, but how far they have developed systems capable of delivering them outside the sub-continent. The three NATO member states, together with Russia, would view with some alarm any attempt by Pakistan (and, perhaps, also India) to acquire ballistic missiles with a range that could reach Paris or New York. The possibility of such a development, and prospects for its prevention, is discussed further in Chapter IV.

Importantly, nuclear restraint at low numbers would not require the degree of intrusive verification likely to be involved in providing assurance of nuclear abolition. Rather, it might be sufficient to put in place information-exchange measures that provided a reasonable degree of assurance against under-announcing of national stockpiles, together with more intensive verification focused on those long- and medium-range ballistic missiles that are operationally available. Nuclear restraint at low numbers would probably also have to include some measures to limit capabilities for missile defence, so that these could not suddenly undermine strategic stability. Information exchanges on stocks of fissile material available for military purposes, and on warhead production facilities, could also add confidence that none of the states could launch a major 'break-out' from low numbers without risking detection.

In contrast to the intrusive measures that would be needed to verify nuclear abolition, the information exchanges associated with nuclear restraint at low numbers would not need to make it impossible for states to hide any warheads. Even so, it must be asked how a state could gain from hiding a stockpile of warheads in an undeclared storage facility. Such undeclared warheads could, by their nature, make no contribution to deterrence if their existence was not suspected; and, even if they were suddenly deployed during a crisis, it is far from clear what additional value they would provide to the country that revealed them. For a possible gain of such doubtful value, moreover, the state embarking on such a concealment exercise would also be taking the risk that it could be found out, with the risks of reputational damage and (at least) political ostracism and sanctions that this could involve.

Deadly Dyads

Even if it is possible to confine the problem in this way, it presents a formidable challenge. In purely arithmetical terms, there are twenty-one potential dyadic relationships between the seven nuclear-armed states. In practice, we can rule out the possibility of nuclear deterrence having a role to play in relations between the US, UK and France; but future arms-restraint regimes must respond to concerns about stability, at least in the long term, in many of the eighteen other dyadic relationships. The four most prominent, and longstanding, of these relationships are between the US and Russia, the US and China, India and Pakistan, and (at least from India's perspective) China and India. Furthermore, while strategic relationships between Russia and China are now relatively friendly, and their past border disputes have been resolved, nuclear stability between these two countries could become more relevant in future, and may be a factor in determining how far Russia (in particular) may be prepared to constrain its nuclear forces.

Prolonged War and Delayed Responses
Proposals for nuclear restraint at low numbers need to accommodate possible unintended consequences. One of these may be a need for military planners to take more seriously the possibility of a protracted conventional war between major powers. In such a conflict, made possible by the states in question refraining from early use of nuclear weapons, concerns over the survivability of nuclear force could increase. For, even if states had secured their nuclear forces against a surprise attack, these forces might still be vulnerable to a prolonged war of attrition.

For example, in a scenario in which the US were to subject Russia or China to a full-scale conventional offensive against its military forces, seeking to destroy command and communication networks as well as key military assets, both countries might fear that their ability to launch a nuclear strike against the US would be steadily eroded over time. The closer that they felt they were to losing this retaliatory capability altogether, the more tempted they would become to threaten escalation to nuclear use if the attack did not cease. In the absence of a prompt nuclear response to the initial large-scale attack, however, the US might misjudge its opponent's resolve to escalate when its nuclear capability was threatened, hoping to finish off its nuclear force before it took this fatal step.

Such a 'prolonged war' scenario – which, given modern military technology, might still last only a matter of weeks or months – illustrates vividly why it will never be possible to put 'nuclear stability' into a separate box, and then assume that conventional war could proceed as if nuclear weapons did not exist. Instead, the existence of nuclear weapons – even in a 'recessed' or 'restrained' configuration – is likely to cast a continuing shadow over any major war, increasing the pressure on all participants to avoid such a war, and to terminate it as quickly as possible.

Nuclear restraint at low numbers may be able to reduce the risk of rapid escalation to nuclear conflict in the first hours of a war; but it cannot eliminate the risk of such a conflict as long as large-scale war between the nuclear-armed states remains a real possibility. Even if all nuclear weapons were eliminated – withdrawn from service and verifiably dismantled – the possibility of their re-creation could still have some deterrent effect. The world's first nuclear weapons were developed from an idea on paper to an operational device within the space of four years between 1941 and 1945. Even if all states had abandoned covert stockpiles and production capabilities, the time from 'blueprint to bomb' would be much shorter today. Some argue, for example, that it could take Japan four years to build operational nuclear weapons if it were to decide to do so.[43] In the middle of a major war, however, this timescale would likely be

---

[43] For a discussion of this point, see Shashank Joshi, 'Japan and the Bomb', *shashankjoshi.wordpress.com*, 29 March 2012.

dramatically shortened, perhaps to a period measured in a few months. The possibility of such a 'reconstitution race' is often given as a further reason why nuclear abolition would not be desirable, unless and until there is a further deep demilitarisation of security relations between the major powers.

Consideration of a 'prolonged war' scenario, however, also focuses attention on another aspect of mutual restraint at low numbers. Traditional nuclear planning, at least in the US and Russia, prioritises the need to be able to use nuclear weapons at short notice in a crisis, since it is assumed that a political crisis could escalate to threatened use of nuclear weapons in a matter of hours or days. Yet a nuclear doctrine based on maintaining a capability for assured retaliation need not necessarily require a capability for prompt response. Provided that an opponent believes that it faces an increased risk of nuclear attack if it takes offensive action of its own, the probability of such retaliation may matter more than its timing. One of the strongest critiques of current US and Russian nuclear postures is that they still rely too heavily on maintaining key missile forces at short notice to fire. This in turn, especially in a crisis, could contribute to an unacceptably high risk that mistakes could be made or accidents could happen.

Yet a deterrent posture based on delayed response need not necessarily imply reduced survivability for strategic forces. One of the reasons that the strategic missile submarines of the US, UK and France are seen as relatively stabilising in strategic terms (compared with silo-based ICBMs, in particular) is that they could 'ride out' a first strike, allowing the national leadership to appraise the nature of any attack and then decide whether or not a retaliatory response would serve any purpose.

Once the potential deterrent value of such a delayed response is acknowledged, however, it opens up new possibilities – as well as challenges – for nuclear-arms restraint, especially for those states which are most concerned about the first-strike capabilities of potential opponents. It means that relatively weak states may want to be able to rely on well-concealed 'bombs in the basement' as an ultimate underpinning of their deterrent, even if they are not available for immediate use. This therefore means that such states are likely to resist too close an accounting for the location of every last nuclear warhead. For, especially in relation to weapons that could only be used at considerable notice, lack of transparency is the best guarantee of survivability. If nuclear restraint at low numbers is to be achieved even in the face of considerable disparities in conventional capabilities, therefore, the answer may lie in focusing both restraint and transparency on those systems that are of most relevant to short-notice attack, while subjecting such 'long-fuse' capabilities to less stringent, but still confidence-building, restraint.

Doomsday Alliances

Proposals for nuclear restraint at low numbers are sometimes seen as particularly problematic, given the possibility that triangular dynamics may become more important in a world where several states possess arsenals of comparable size. Two scenarios could, in principle, present themselves.

The first is a 'mutual exhaustion' scenario, in which two nuclear-armed states exhaust themselves in a nuclear exchange, allowing a third power to move into the vacuum that they have left. Such is the scenario that the Soviet Union might have envisaged in Europe after 1939, for example, with Stalin hoping that the democratic and fascist powers would fight each other to a standstill, allowing his forces to expand into Europe as liberators. Had it not been for US intervention, Japan might have hoped for a similar outcome in the Pacific, with European withdrawal from Asia as a result of German advances leaving Southeast Asia open to its advancing troops.

It is far less clear, however, that such a scenario (in either a conventional or nuclear form) is plausible today. The instinct for territorial annexation, so powerful in the imperial age, has more or less disappeared from the calculus of the major powers, and recent US and NATO experiences in Iraq and Afghanistan have provided a fresh reminder (if one were needed) of the considerable costs (and limited economic benefits) of even temporary occupation.

Furthermore, while a major India-Pakistan war remains a possibility – with many in Pakistan believing India might attempt to change Pakistan's borders by force, and many Indians expressing concern that Pakistan might capitalise on an India-China war to settle old scores[44] – it is hard to see how any third power would benefit in such a war's aftermath. Neither China nor the US would, for one moment, be interested in moving in to colonise the devastated post-nuclear cities of South Asia. The main problem, instead, would be to mobilise the international resources that would be needed to respond to the massive humanitarian consequences – including international refugee flows – that would follow a nuclear war. One could, just about, imagine a more adventurist and nationalistic China taking advantage of a disarmed India in order to annex those areas currently occupied by India (notably Arunachal Pradesh) to which it has long laid claim. However, it would have powerful reasons not to do so, given the strong reactions that this could trigger from other Asian and world powers. In contrast to the pre-1939 world, a broad coalition of democratic powers, led by the US but including most of the world's strongest states, continues to play a key role in shaping and enforcing international norms, one of the most powerful of which is the injunction against changing borders by force. Any attempt to substantially subvert

---

[44] James M Acton, *Deterrence During Disarmament*, p. 88.

such a norm in a period of nuclear crisis could risk triggering strong counter-measures – economic, political and military – from this coalition.

A second, and perhaps less implausible, scenario is that one of the nuclear-armed states might face a combined threat from several others. This is what the Soviet Union proposed to the US in 1969, when it was contemplating a pre-emptive attack on China's small nuclear force.[45] The most plausible current scenario in this category today is that the three NATO Nuclear-Weapon States would combine forces (as they are obliged to do through the North Atlantic Treaty) in the face of a future nuclear threat from Russia, or (possibly) China, or (just possibly) Pakistan. If such an alliance were to produce a credible first-strike option that the US could not provide on its own, it would indeed be a source of legitimate concern. However, a shift from a policy of overwhelming destruction to one of guaranteed, but less destabilising, response could help to mitigate this concern.

One of the challenges in mutual restraint at low numbers, therefore, would be how to respect the autonomy of each of the NATO Nuclear-Weapon States while also enabling the UK and France to reassure others that they are contributing to the success of this process. Both countries are likely to resist being placed in permanently numerical inferiority compared with other nuclear-armed states: that would be a perverse penalty for countries that are in alliance with each other. However, it would be reasonable to ask both countries to be prepared to reduce their operational arsenals significantly below current levels, in the event that other nuclear-armed states – and Russia in particular – were prepared to cut their arsenals down to the low hundreds.

To Zero and Beyond

Must the process of nuclear disarmament stop when arsenals are reduced to low numbers? Popular support for the goal of universal nuclear disarmament remains as strong as ever, in nuclear-armed and Non-Nuclear-Weapon States, amongst political and military elites as well as the general population. This support derives much of its strength from the wider, albeit incomplete, pacification of relations between the major powers, and from a strong moral prohibition against the use (and, to a lesser extent, testing) of nuclear weapons. It is strengthened by a sense that an international regime that is based on inequality between nuclear 'haves' and nuclear 'have-nots' cannot be sustained forever in a world where new powers are increasingly seeking a role as active players in world politics,

---

[45] Michael S Gerson, *The Sino-Soviet Border Conflict: Deterrence, Escalation and the Threat of Nuclear War in 1969* (Alexandria, VA: Center for Naval Analyses, November 2010).

alongside the five great powers that emerged at the end of the Second World War. Moreover, at least for now, it is sustained by the success of the international community in slowing the pace of nuclear proliferation. Iran may yet, however, be the straw that breaks that particular back, on which the fate of the global non-proliferation regime rests.

If relations between the world's major powers were to improve to the extent that war between them was no more likely than it is between the US and Canada, or between France and Germany, then the combined political weight of the major powers might be enough to compel lesser powers to give up their remaining arsenals in return for credible security guarantees. In these circumstances, complete nuclear disarmament might be attainable even if there remained a residual risk that a rogue state or terrorist might one day re-acquire a nuclear capability. As long as other major powers (such as Russia and China) have nuclear weapons, however, it would be neither desirable nor feasible for the US to give up its own forces unilaterally. Even if it were to do so, the world would not suddenly see an aggressive rush for world domination. There are too many other disincentives – domestic and international – for that to happen. However, it would risk the development of new instabilities, not least because it would focus increased attention on the potential use of nuclear weapons for coercion, rather than continuing the trend towards reducing their role in security relationships.

Within the broad framework set out in this section, the next chapter will seek to describe in more detail a definition of, and the issues surrounding, mutual restraint at low numbers. It is not designed to be a rigid prescription, in which the reader is asked to accept every element in a comprehensive blueprint for what the nuclear order should look like in 2030. Its aim is more modest and heuristic. The preparation of this paper will have been worthwhile if it can stimulate further thinking as to where the processes of nuclear-arms control and restraint should go next, especially if the world begins to move into a period when a wider range of nuclear-armed states are being urged to take part in the process.

IV. THE JIGSAW OF RESTRAINT

The wider objective of mutual nuclear restraint would be to create a state of affairs in which all seven of the acknowledged nuclear-armed states were reasonably satisfied that the size and shape of their nuclear arsenals were sufficient for their own security purposes, and to do so through a process of draw-down in the forces of the US and Russia, rather than through build-up by China, India and Pakistan. It would involve the nuclear-armed states each having no more than 500 operationally available warheads, with most having significantly fewer than this. The total number of nuclear weapons in national arsenals would thus be reduced to around 2,000, compared to today's total of 11,500, with the remaining warheads removed and designated for dismantlement. A parallel process of non-proliferation policies would continue to seek to prevent, contain or reverse the emergence of new nuclear-armed states (such as Iran and North Korea).

The package of understandings and agreements that would underpin such a reduction would need to be constructed so as to ensure that each of the seven nuclear-armed states felt that its own particular concerns had been addressed, and that it did not feel worse off than it would be without mutual restraint. Its design would therefore have to weigh carefully two balances.

First, in addition to restraining nuclear arsenals themselves, it would need to develop a regime of restraint in relation to other capabilities that also contribute to strategic nuclear relationships, such as those for missile defence and conventional strike. Due to the central role that survivability plays in ensuring mutual vulnerability, this implies a strong focus on both ballistic missiles and systems designed to combat them. These capabilities have been central to relationships between the nuclear powers since the early 1960s, and remain central to concerns about second-strike stability. As US capabilities in missile defence and conventionally armed ballistic missiles continue to develop, it is not practical to examine requirements for restraint at low numbers without taking them into account.

Second, a balance would need to be struck between focusing on those systems that are particularly important for ensuring second-strike stability – such as warheads deployed on long-range ballistic missiles and associated defensive systems – and also taking into account the capabilities for future 'break-out' represented by less immediately useable second-echelon capabilities, such as weapons in storage, military-grade fissile material, and factories for fissile material, warhead and missile production.

The main focus for restraint in the coming period should be long-range ballistic missiles, together with those warheads that are deployed for use on them, given the particular risk that they are often seen as posing to mutual vulnerability, especially at low numbers. Fortunately, this is also the main principle underpinning current US-Russia nuclear arms-limitation treaties. These treaties – and in particular the New START and INF Treaties – already provide detailed definitions of limited systems, rules for counting these systems when deployed, and mechanisms for verifying national declarations. These arrangements will have to be amended and extended to remain relevant at much lower levels of US and Russian nuclear forces, and to take account of other systems that only the other nuclear-armed states possess. Nevertheless, they provide an excellent starting point, of relevance both to the next stage of US-Russia reductions and to the first steps through which the other five states might become involved in the process.

At the same time, as total numbers of US and Russian deployed weapons fall, it would also be important to provide some measure of reassurance in relation to second-echelon capabilities. A sustainable arrangement would have to reassure each of the nuclear-armed states that any potential adversary was not hiding a capability that enabled it covertly to double or triple the size of its operational arsenal at short notice. The suspected existence of such a capability, without any countervailing confidence-building and transparency measures, could undermine the credibility of counting rules focused solely on 'first-echelon', deployed forces. It could also lead to fears that a state hiding such forces was intent on maintaining a capability to subvert the nuclear balance, using its greater ability to 'break out' as a means of exercising leverage in a future crisis. Such fears should not be overstated. If remaining deployed arsenals number in the hundreds, and are also reasonably survivable, the operational advantages of such 'break-out' capabilities would be slim.

It would be important to ask all nuclear-armed states to provide enough information on these capabilities so as to provide a clear, and regularly updated, picture of their scale and significance; but it would not be necessary to require the same levels of intrusive verification as is currently provided for New START limited systems. Such 'appropriate transparency' for second-echelon capabilities should be enough to ensure that no state could gain political advantage from hinting at the existence of much bigger forces. Over time, moreover, confidence would be likely to grow in the accuracy of mutual understandings of these capabilities, helping to reduce the extent to which this was a factor in limiting the cuts made to operational arsenals.

In the initial stages of moving towards a situation in which none of the nuclear-armed states had more than 500 operational nuclear weapons, however, the existence of second-echelon capabilities could have a further, and to some extent contradictory, benefit. It would allow those states which are most worried by the conventional edge (including missile defence) possessed by potential rivals to retain an important element of hedging in their own force postures. If they felt the need to do so, states could protect and conceal these additional capabilities (including weapons in storage, together with fissile material that could be used to construct new weapons within weeks) so as to make them harder to target in the event of an enemy first strike, especially in countries (such as Russia and China) that can use bases far from their international borders.

No nuclear aggressor, therefore, could gamble that such a delayed retaliatory response would be rendered impossible, even if it did think that it had the capability for disarming or intercepting the first-echelon systems that would be the retaliatory systems of choice. In order to protect such capabilities in the first stages of moving to restraint at low numbers, appropriate verification might include clear declarations as to their maximum size. Such statements could, for example, include: 'no more than 200 warheads in storage'; 'no more than 10 stockpiled tonnes of plutonium and/or highly enriched uranium'; 'no more than 5 tonnes of [highly enriched uranium] for use in submarine reactors'. However, some continuing ambiguity in relation to the precise size and location of such stockpiles would still be allowed – and this could then be progressively narrowed, if and when confidence grew that increased transparency would not undermine national security.

This model for focused restraint and appropriate transparency differs significantly from what would be required for complete nuclear disarmament. If an abolition agreement were reached, it would require verification measures that ensured not only that all existing nuclear weapons had been dismantled, but also that transparency in relation to fissile material and military infrastructure was intensive enough to ensure that new weapons could not quickly be reconstructed.[1]

What matters at low numbers, by contrast, is to avoid creating a situation in which any country fears that a potential opponent might consider a disarming first strike. This requirement is likely to be the main

---

[1] For a thoughtful account of what an agreement on nuclear disarmament might contain, together with the associated information exchange and verification requirements, see George Perkovich and James M Acton, *Abolishing Nuclear Weapons*, Adelphi Paper 396 (Abingdon: Routledge for IISS, August 2008).

driver for the lower limit of agreement regarding the size of offensive arsenals, and also points to the need for restraint and predictability in relation to other capabilities, including missile defences. However, it also means, as argued above, that 'full' transparency may not always be desirable, especially where some countries believe that opacity (especially in second-echelon capabilities) can contribute to deterrence of a disarming first strike.

Some resistance to such suggestions might be expected from those who see mutual restraint at low numbers solely through the lens of creating the conditions for rapid transition to abolition, and who therefore do not believe that it is necessary to create conditions for stability at intermediate stages. Indeed, some of the strongest criticism of mutual restraint could come from those who worry about any arrangement that might be seen as legitimating a deterrent role for nuclear weapons at this stage, thereby diverting political attention from the ultimate objective of complete disarmament.

Those who believe that the main priority should be to create conditions for a rapid move to nuclear abolition might also have a mixed reaction to the argument that mutual deterrence could be enhanced by the belief that other powers might still possess 'recessed' or hidden nuclear capabilities. They might worry that the possible existence of such capabilities could make the verification challenges involved in abolition even harder. On the other hand, it might add weight to the argument that, even if a negotiated and verifiable dismantlement of all nuclear weapons could be achieved, the possibility that such capabilities could be recreated in future would constitute a form of 'weaponless deterrence' regardless.[2]

As a matter of practical international politics, however, it is hard to imagine that today's nuclear-armed states would be prepared to move directly to abolition without passing through an extended period of restraint at low numbers, during which they can assess their potential foes' intentions and capabilities in a less-nuclear environment, and determine whether it would be in their interests to take the final step towards complete abolition.

Three Elements in a Package of Bilateral Restraint

While further reductions in the arsenals of the US and Russia are likely whatever happens, a more deliberate package of measures and agreements will be needed in order for the two countries to move

---

[2] For an early discussion, see Jonathan Schell, *The Abolition* (New York: Knopf, 1984). For a recent analysis, see Christopher Ford, 'Nuclear Weapons Reconstitution and its Discontents: Challenges of "Weaponless Deterrence"', Hudson Institute, November 2010.

towards postures in which mutual restraint by all the nuclear-armed states becomes a relevant proposition. Such a package is likely to involve three key dimensions, each of which is related to the others, but not all of which would have to be agreed or implemented simultaneously. First, it would involve substantial reductions in numbers of those delivery systems and deployed warheads counted under New START. Second, it would probably have to involve confidence-building and restraint measures in relation to strategic conventional capabilities, particularly in relation to US missile defence capabilities. Third, it would have to include restraint and transparency in relation to 'second-echelon' nuclear capabilities, including warheads not counted in New START, stockpiles of fissile material, and other elements that support deployed nuclear forces.

Once the US and Russia are on course to make further reductions in their own arsenals, and in order to encourage them to do more, the smaller nuclear-armed states would also need to adopt restraint and confidence-building measures, as discussed in the second part of this chapter.

In the discussion that follows, a key distinctive theme is the need for reduction and restraint measures to be co-ordinated but also reversible, at least initially. The traditional model of arms control places considerable emphasis on the need for legally binding agreements, whether these are bilateral (the New START agreement and the now-expired ABM Treaty) or multilateral (the CTBT, and the proposed Fissile Material Cut-off Treaty [FMCT]).[3] While such agreements have a place in the panoply of arms restraint, however, there is a risk that placing too much weight on such legally binding measures may limit the potential for more flexible processes of mutual concession. This risk is likely to increase if further states begin to join the restraint process. In leaving open the possibility of reversibility, the states involved in a multilateral process would be recognising the reality that, in a world of sovereign states, there is a limit to the value of international security agreements in any case. As importantly, a model for mutual restraint that does not involve a single 'grand treaty' may be more acceptable to states that want to hedge against the possibility of adverse strategic developments even as they seek to embark on a process of confidence-building that could make these developments less likely.

The First Element: Building on New START
There is already a well-established framework for restrictions on the nuclear arsenals of the US and Russia, beginning with SALT 1 signed by President Nixon and General Secretary Leonid Brezhnev in May 1972. This

---

[3] For an example of such an approach, see Richard Burt and Jan Lodal, 'The Next Step for Arms Control: A Nuclear Control Regime', *Survival* (Vol. 53, No. 6, December 2011), pp. 51–72.

was succeeded by the 1979 SALT 2 Treaty (not submitted for US Senate ratification as a result of the Soviet invasion of Afghanistan, but observed by both sides) and the 1991 START Treaty (START 1), which entered into force in December 1994 and limited both sides to no more than 6,000 warheads on 1,600 delivery vehicles. A further important landmark was the 1987 INF Treaty, which prohibited both the US and the Soviet Union (now Russia) from possessing or deploying any ground-based missiles (conventional or nuclear) with a range of between 500 km and 5,500 km.

Under President George W Bush, an effort was made to shift nuclear arms reductions to a less formal model. The 2002 SORT Treaty (Strategic Offensive Reductions Treaty), also known as the Moscow Treaty, limited both sides to having no more than 2,200 warheads, but added no new verification provisions to those already in force as a result of the START 1 Treaty.

Most recently, Presidents Obama and Medvedev signed the New START Treaty in April 2010, which entered into force in February 2011. The new treaty limits the number of deployed warheads to 1,550 from 2018 onwards, and also limits the number of deployed long-range missiles and heavy bombers to 700. A further limit of 800 is imposed on the total number of deployed and un-deployed delivery vehicles (missiles and heavy bombers), in order to allow for weapons held in store or for conventional purposes. Detailed arrangements have been made for information exchange and on-site verification measures to ensure that both sides are satisfied that the other is abiding by its commitments.

Focusing on Ballistic Missiles:
One of the key principles of the New START Treaty, as in the START 1 Treaty that preceded it, focuses on the need to limit the number of long-range ballistic missiles and the nuclear weapons deployed on them. In part, this derives from verification considerations: ICBMs and SLBMs (submarine-launched ballistic missiles), together with the facilities required to make them operational, are large and hard to conceal. However, it also coincides with stability considerations, with 'fast-flying', long-range missiles seen as more likely to be useful in a surprise attack than the 'slow-flying', shorter-range cruise missiles (or gravity bombs) that are deployed on long-range bombers.

As a consequence, even when heavy bombers are capable of carrying up to twenty warheads apiece, each bomber is counted as being equivalent to only one warhead for New START purposes. This single device has been estimated to undercount current (2010) US-deployed warheads by 450 and Russian-deployed warheads by 860.[4] It has the

---

[4] Hans M Kristensen, 'New START Treaty Has New Counting', *fas.org*, 29 March 2010.

advantage, however, of avoiding the difficulties that would be involved in verifying numbers of warheads when (as is now generally the case) they are not deployed on board the aircraft in question. This, together with their long flight time compared with ballistic missiles, means that heavy bombers are less effective in a first-strike threat role.[5]

In the aftermath of the New START Treaty, both the US and Russia have sought to widen the scope of the next round of reductions. The US Senate, in its Consent to Ratification, insisted that the US government should 'seek to initiate, following consultation with NATO allies but not later than one year after the entry into force of the New START Treaty, negotiations with the Russian Federation on an agreement to address the disparity between the non-strategic (tactical) nuclear-weapons stockpiles of the Russian Federation and of the United States and to secure and reduce tactical nuclear weapons in a verifiable manner'.[6] Russia, for its part, has argued that a new treaty would also have to limit US deployment of strategic missile defences, a suggestion that the US is vigorously resisting.

Yet both these areas – 'tactical' nuclear weapons and missile defences – are characterised by asymmetry between US and Russian capabilities (with Russia having more deployed tactical nuclear weapons and the US developing a growing lead in deployed missile defences). Other elements – such as the US's larger number of reserve warheads for 'upload' onto its under-loaded ballistic missiles, or Russia's greater capabilities for warhead production – could also be brought into the picture. By widening negotiations prematurely to include some or all of these capabilities, however, the two countries could find themselves spending several years unnecessarily deadlocked in discussions on secondary concerns. If strategic arsenals are to be reduced to much lower levels, transparency and confidence-building measures in relation to both missile defences and those capabilities not counted by New START will ultimately be desirable. At this stage, however, there is probably more that can be done in relation to strategic arsenals without resolving the difficult issues – not least in relation to verification – that such expansion would involve.

The Existing Gap

In particular, there is more that can be done relatively quickly, by operating, within the framework of the existing New START agreement, to drive the

---

[5] US Department of Defense, 'Nuclear Posture Review Report 2010', April 2010, p. 21.
[6] US Department of State, 'New START Treaty: Resolution of Advice and Instrument of Ratification', 22 December 2010, <http://www.state.gov/t/avc/rls/153910.htm>, accessed 13 August 2012.

Table 2: Deployed Strategic Forces, April 2012.

	Russia	United States	New START 2018 Limit
Total deployed delivery vehicles	494	812	**700**
Total deployed warheads*	1,492	1,737	**1,550**

Source: US State Department Bureau of Arms Control, Verification and Compliance, 'New START Treaty Aggregate Numbers of Strategic Offensive Arms', Fact Sheet, 6 April 2012; Hans M Kristensen and Robert S Norris, 'Russian Nuclear Forces, 2012', *Bulletin of the Atomic Scientists* (Vol. 68, No. 2, 2012); Hans M Kristensen and Robert S Norris, 'US Nuclear Forces, 2011', *Bulletin of the Atomic Scientists* (Vol. 67, No. 2, 2011).
*Under New START counting rules, each heavy bomber is counted as carrying only one deployed warhead.

Table 3: Trends in US and Russian Strategic Forces.

	1988	2012
US SSBNs	36	12
Soviet Union/Russian SSBNs	62	9
US SLBMs	640	249
Soviet Union/Russian SLBMs	942	144
US heavy bombers	337	125
Soviet Union/Russian heavy bombers	175	72
US ICBMs	1,000	448
Soviet Union/Russian ICBMs	1,386	322

Sources: IISS, *The Military Balance 1988–89*, Autumn 1998, pp. 18, 33–24; US State Department Bureau of Arms Control, Verification and Compliance, 'New START Treaty Aggregate Numbers of Strategic Offensive Arms', Fact Sheet, 6 April 2012.

mutual reductions process forward by several more steps. The starting point for such a process should be a more explicit recognition, by both countries, that the treaty provides ceilings for strategic arsenals, but it does not provide floors.

As of early 2012, Russia already had rather fewer warheads (1,492) than the number (1,550) which it will be allowed when the treaty's limits fully come into force in 2018. It also has far fewer delivery vehicles (a total of 494) than the treaty allows (700). In its effort to maintain rough parity with the US in terms of numbers of deployed warheads, despite its more limited economic resources, Russia has focused its efforts on multiple-warhead ICBMs, while saving money by making sharp reductions in numbers of missiles and missile submarines.

By contrast, more funding has been made available in the US's defence budget over the last two decades to pay for the maintenance and deployment of a large arsenal of missiles, missile submarines and heavy bombers, as Table 2 shows. While the size of its nuclear force, as measured by missiles and bombers, has fallen since the end of the Cold War, the reduction has been significantly less steep than in the Soviet Union/Russia. As a result, the US now has more SSBNs (ballistic missile submarines), more SLBMs and ICBMs and more nuclear-armed strategic bombers than does Russia.

The Nuclear Posture Review has made it clear that the US will meet its New START obligations by reducing numbers of deployed missiles and warheads to the required ceilings. The Nuclear Posture Review Implementation Study could accelerate this process. However, depending on the outcome of this review, there will be more that could be done to create the conditions for mutual restraint at low numbers, without a new treaty and without (at this stage) requiring that all the other nuclear-armed states agree to restrain their own, much smaller, forces.

Making Sharp, but Reversible, Reductions
In particular, there is a strong case for considering the feasibility of embarking on a process of repeated reciprocal reductions that would reduce the strategic arsenals of both the US and Russia to around half the levels of deployed warheads set in the New START Treaty (in round terms, 750 each), and to do so before the end of the decade. An interim target set at this level would still leave both countries with a number of deployed warheads that is more than twice the total nuclear stockpile of any of the other nuclear-armed states. By reducing the number of their most significant strategic weapons to well below 1,000 deployed warheads each, the US and Russia could begin to make a case for other nuclear-armed states to restrict their own capabilities. This new level, on the other hand, should still be high enough to assuage Russia's concerns about the impact of US missile defences and conventional strike forces on its second-strike capability (at least for the next decade or so). Importantly, it would also be high enough to ensure that neither side would be seen as gaining significant 'first-strike' advantage from covertly uploading its missiles during a crisis.

It will not be easy to strike a balance between these competing factors, and a 50 per cent reduction in US and Russian deployed strategic arsenals may still not be enough to entice other states into the process. The US possesses large stockpiles of reserve strategic missile warheads, and this number might initially increase in the event of rapid reductions in deployed warheads. Russia, for its part, is thought to have around 1,000 operational non-strategic (shorter-range) nuclear weapons while the US has around 500 weapons in this category, including 150–200 deployed in Europe. Due to New START counting rules, moreover, both countries still have several hundred warheads stored at strategic bomber bases, but not included in the declared total.

Even after a reduction to fewer than 1,000 deployed strategic warheads each, therefore, the two countries could still be left with total operational stockpiles in excess of 2,000 warheads, at least five times larger than those of either France or China. Furthermore, this total would not include the large number of warheads 'awaiting dismantlement', currently in excess of 3,000 for both countries, which is likely to remain high well into the 2020s.

While such large second-echelon arsenals will make it hard to convince the smaller nuclear-armed states to accept lower limits on their own forces, however, they should make it easier for the US and Russia to agree to sharp reductions in their strategic arsenals. Under the reciprocation scenario under discussion, no new legally binding treaty would be agreed. Both sides would therefore retain the right to reload warheads onto existing missiles, or to deploy new missiles, if they chose to do so, up to New START ceilings. Rather than maintaining large numbers of warheads in active deployment as a hedge against possible future risks, however, any reserve forces that the US or Russia felt necessary to maintain would be kept at a lower state of readiness. Such 'hedge' forces would not be structured for mobilisation in times of crisis. Rather, they would allow states to maintain a medium-term option, within, say, two to five years, of deploying additional capabilities in response to the emergence of new and unexpected threats (such as greatly improved missile defences or nano-technology-based drone strike capabilities) that threatened the viability of a smaller deployed force.

Such a posture might, for example, help provide Russia's leaders with assurance that they could deploy a timely response were the US (perhaps a decade from now) to begin to field large-scale strategic missile defences capable of rendering a Russian second strike considerably less effective. Yet, as discussed below, the chances of the US developing such a capability are greatly overstated. As long as such a US capability is not deployed, therefore, there would be no need for Russia to reverse the reduction process. Confidence-building measures in relation to US missile defences could further diminish the need to retain a large Russian 'hedge' force. Provided that other nuclear-armed states (such as China) show that they are satisfied with relatively small arsenals, Russia could also be convinced that the level of deployed capability necessary to deter US aggression is much smaller than had previously been the basis for its force planning.

Retaining the option of reconstituting its deployed strategic forces at higher levels might also help to persuade US sceptics. The US has even less need to worry about the destabilising consequences of lower numbers than Russia, given the invulnerability of its SLBMs and the limited scale of Russian missile defences. For, as long as these factors remain, the US could maintain the ability to inflict unacceptable damage on Russia (or any other country) with an arsenal consisting of as few as 200 deployed submarine-based warheads.

Russia does maintain a large, though uncertain, numerical superiority in NSNW. Until recently, however, conservative US experts usually dismissed this margin as being largely irrelevant to the strategic balance because of their limited range and capabilities. One of President George W Bush's most influential advisers, Robert Joseph, for example, has argued that 'Russia's theater nuclear weapons, even if modernized, will not give Moscow the capability to alter the strategic landscape...Russia's theater nuclear weapons are not...destabilizing.'[7] It is significant that this view runs contrary to the position taken by Republican leaders in the US Senate, who insisted that the administration press for inclusion of these weapons in future negotiations as a condition for ratification of New START.

Avoiding Omnibus Negotiations
Strong support for widening the next round of negotiations to include NSNW has also come from those focused on the need to create the conditions for complete nuclear disarmament. At this stage of the disarmament process, however, such a widening would be premature, and could serve to block further progress towards mutual restraint at low numbers. The US and Russia could launch 'omnibus' negotiations, and seek to encompass New START systems and NSNW, reload and bomber warheads, missile defence and conventional strike in an all-or-nothing attempt at reaching a 'grand bargain'. The result, however, would almost certainly be 'nothing'. Given the distinct nature of the problems under each of these headings, it would be much better to pursue these tracks separately for now. At much lower numbers, these tracks do become increasingly interdependent. Unless and until US and Russian strategic arsenals have come down to levels well below 1,000 warheads, however, tight linkages between these different tracks would be counterproductive.

Making the First Step
Since it currently maintains warhead and delivery-system deployments significantly larger than those of Russia, the US should be willing to take the first step in this process, making it clear that, first, it will rapidly reduce its number of New START-counted warheads from its current (April 2012)

---

[7] Robert Joseph, 'Nuclear Weapons and Regional Deterrence', in Jeffrey A Larson and Kurt J Klingenberger (eds.), *Controlling Non-strategic Nuclear Weapons: Obstacles and Opportunities* (United States Air Force, Institute for National Security Studies, July 2001), p. 90, cited in Amy F Woolf, 'Nonstrategic Nuclear Weapons', Congressional Research Service, 12 February 2012, p. 28.

level of 1,737 to a level comparable to that of Russia, at 1,492; and secondly, it would be willing to make further sharp reductions in the size of its deployed arsenal, in parallel with similar reductions by Russia, at least down to a level around half of the current New START warhead ceiling.

Were such a process to take place, the US could choose to reduce its deployed warhead arsenal entirely through a process of 'de-MIRVing' – removing warheads from multiple-warhead, SLBMs – but making no reduction in its total number of deployed missiles and bombers below the number (700) to which it is required to reduce by 2018 under New START. However, this could be a missed opportunity, both for financial and arms-restraint reasons. The US currently fields a fleet of strategic missiles and bombers that is 65 per cent larger (at 812) than that deployed by Russia (currently 494). It also deploys twelve ballistic missile submarines, compared to the nine deployed by Russia. So the political requirement to preserve numerical parity with Russia is not a constraining factor here, at least in relation to some modest initial reductions. Moreover, by making reductions in missile numbers that are comparable to those in warheads, the US could help assuage Russian concerns over the US's greater capabilities for 'uploading' additional warheads onto its missiles. The US could also begin to make some significant financial savings, for example if it were able to withdraw two or three of its oldest *Ohio*-class missile submarines from service, and thereby delay its programme for a new generation of replacement boats.

A process of reciprocal reductions down to around 700–800 deployed strategic warheads apiece by the end of the decade would be an opportunity for both countries to begin to shift the focus of their deterrent doctrines, and associated force structures, towards the 'minimum deterrent' postures associated with the smaller nuclear-armed states. It might mean, for example, removing from service most of the forces – such as silo-based ICBMs – that make least sense in a purely second-strike role.

Russia's Role
Russia's contribution to a reciprocal reduction process could also be achieved, if it decided to do so, by focusing on cuts in the number of warheads carried on each of its long-range missiles. Russia currently deploys an average of three warheads per strategic delivery vehicle, compared with just over two for the US. Such a focus would narrow this gap. This option might be particularly attractive to military commanders who want to build a greater 'upload' capability, more comparable to that already possessed by the US. It would also have considerable appeal to missile producers, with whom President Putin has recently confirmed plans for the production of 400 new, long-range missiles (ICBM and SLBM) over the next decade.

Russia could have strong economic incentives to put more of the weight of reductions on missile numbers. It is already struggling to maintain its arsenal of long-range missiles at current numbers, and analysts expect the total to fall further over the next decade, whether or not further reciprocal reductions take place. Russia could therefore choose to accompany a reduction in deployed warheads to 750 with a further reduction in deployed long-range missiles, perhaps to as low as 250 if it were to maintain current warhead loadings. Given its continuing concerns over a possible US first strike, however, together with its desire to maintain missile-production capabilities, it is likely to be reluctant to go too far down this road.

Even this reduced arsenal would still leave Russia with many times more strategic missiles than China (with an estimated inventory of forty ICBMs), France (with forty-eight deployed SLBMs) and the UK (with forty-eight deployed SLBMs, now being reduced to twenty-four).[8] Furthermore, like the US, Russia would still reserve the right to increase its arsenal in the event of adverse strategic developments, such as the much-feared – but also much postponed – US BMD breakthrough.

The interim proposal outlined here – reciprocal US-Russia reductions to half the current New START ceiling – intentionally focuses on those systems which could potentially pose the greatest risks to second-strike stability, and for which verification mechanisms have also been agreed. The proposal is designed to be self-standing, and capable of implementation within a short period of years if the governments of the US and Russia were to agree to take it forward.

A Second Round of Reductions
Provided that satisfactory progress was being made on the other dimensions of restraint discussed below – missile defences, second-echelon capabilities (including NSNW), and assurances by other nuclear-armed states – it would then be reasonable to ask both the US and Russia to move towards adopting strategic nuclear postures similar to the 'minimum-deterrent' postures that China, France and the UK currently have. In order to reduce first-strike risks in such a low-numbers scenario, it would be desirable for the proportionate reduction in US and Russian weapons platforms – especially boats and aircraft – to be less than that in deployed strategic warheads.

---

[8] Some experts have argued that, if New START definitions are used, China currently has no 'deployed' strategic missiles. For the purposes of the comparison made here, however, Russia would be interested in the number that China could deploy at short notice.

Even with this proviso, the US could still, for example, reduce its SSBN fleet to five or six deployed boats with forty warheads on each (the level to which the UK is now committed to reducing its own SSBN warhead loading). Further SSBNs could be in the operational cycle, but without being deployed. In one scenario, the US could still maintain an ICBM force and a fleet of flexible, nuclear-capable aircraft, with the latter in particular having a potential role as a surge capability.

Alternatively, in order to retain the ability to maintain an effective two-ocean SSBN fleet, the US could maintain a ten-boat submarine force but reduce the number of deployed warheads in each boat to around 30, dismantle its ICBM force altogether – the force element least capable of surviving a first strike – and sharply reduce the nuclear loading of its bombers.[9]

Russia could make reductions of comparable magnitude, but probably with more emphasis on retaining mobile, single-warhead ICBM forces, given the rather greater vulnerabilities of its missile submarines. It might also follow the US in closing one of its two, expensive, missile submarine bases. Concerns over vulnerability to US (or indeed future Chinese) anti-submarine warfare capabilities might, however, stay Russia's hand on this more than it would that of the US.

The Politics of Reductions

In order for the US and Russia to reduce their deployed strategic arsenals to levels more comparable with those of the smaller nuclear-armed states, much more will have to be done to build assurances of restraint in relation to strategic missile defences, second-echelon nuclear capabilities, and (not least) the nuclear programmes of other states. However, the biggest obstacles to such reductions remain within the US and Russia themselves; and these obstacles lie primarily in the realms of domestic politics, rather than in any good operational or strategic reasons for needing vastly larger arsenals than other major powers. In the process of building massive arsenals during the Cold War, and doing so at enormous expense, both countries have also accrued strategic cultures, doctrines and powerful vested interests, each of which acts to slow the pace at which the two countries are prepared to change. Nevertheless, they have changed. Throughout the two decades since the end of the Cold War, the nuclear

---

[9] The report of the Global Zero US Nuclear Policy Commission, which was chaired by former Vice-Chair of the Joint Chiefs of Staff James Cartwright, proposes a total force of 450 deployed warheads, including ten missile submarines with 360 deployed warheads, together with eighteen B-2 bombers with ninety deployed warheads. A further 450 warheads would be held in reserve. Global Zero US Nuclear Policy Commission, 'Modernizing U.S. Nuclear Strategy, Force Structure and Posture', May 2012, p. 7.

arsenals of both countries have continued to fall, and (even in Russia) the role of nuclear forces in practical defence planning has lessened substantially. Moreover, this change has continued to take place under both Democrat and Republican presidents in the US, and under the leaderships of successive presidents, of very different views, in Russia. Absent a massive deterioration in relations between the two countries – and perhaps even then – the momentum towards a further lowering of numbers can be expected to continue. Whether it can be realised to the extent suggested here, however, remains an open question.

Provided that progress can be made on all the restraint tracks identified here, it would be reasonable to aim to reduce US and Russian total deployed arsenals to no more than 500 warheads each by 2025. Whether this is possible in practice will depend, *inter alia*, on the fulfilment of the three other conditions, which are now examined in turn.

The Second Element: Limiting Missile Defences

Strategic missile defences pose particular problems for the willingness of Russia to move to restraint at low numbers. Indeed, Russia has made clear that it expects the issue of missile defence to form part of the next, post-New START, round of arms-control negotiations.

This is not a new problem. The very first agreement on limiting strategic offensive weapons, the 1972 SALT treaty, was accompanied by the ABM Treaty, which limited the two powers to two interceptor sites each, one for the capital and one for ICBM fields. These restrictions were subsequently revised, in the 1974 protocol, to limit the number of interceptor sites to one each.

From the start, however, a powerful element of US opinion was critical of the acceptance of national vulnerability to nuclear attack that this implied, and argued that the US's ability to defend itself should not be limited in this way. These arguments gained new political credibility as relations between the two superpowers worsened after 1979, especially after President Reagan endorsed plans (put to him by Edward Teller) for a comprehensive 'shield' against ballistic missile attack. Even after relations began to improve post the 1983 Able Archer crisis, and the subsequent elevation of Mikhail Gorbachev to the Soviet leadership, prospects for future US BMD programmes played a key – and negative – role in superpower relations. At the landmark summit in Iceland in 1986, Gorbachev was prepared to accept Reagan's remarkable proposal for the elimination of all nuclear weapons within a decade (including, one presumes, all long-range ballistic missiles); but the sticking point was Gorbachev's insistence that the US stop work on missile defences.

Gorbachev need not have bothered. A quarter of a century later, and despite the removal of ABM Treaty restrictions in 2001, the US is no nearer to the creation of a comprehensive 'Star Wars' missile defence shield than it was at Reykjavik. All it has to show for many billions of dollars of investment is thirty ground-based strategic missile interceptors at two locations: still fewer than the 200 interceptors at two sites (though not the sites in Alaska and California now being used) that would have been allowed under the original ABM Treaty in any case.

Despite its limited achievements so far, however, the US's efforts to develop defences against long-range missiles have continued to be a source of tension with Russia. The decision by President George W Bush to withdraw from the ABM Treaty, in particular, contributed to Russian distrust at a time when relations were already deteriorating in the wake of the Kosovo War and NATO's agreement to enlarge eastwards to include former Soviet allies and republics. This distrust remains to this day, with Russia continuing to insist that it needs legally binding guarantees that the US will not deploy missile defences directed against its own strategic forces, and the US reluctant to do so.

The Shadow of the Future
The problem does not lie with existing US capabilities, or even those being planned for deployment during the next decade. Even in its most effective fourth phase, due for deployment by 2020, the European Phased Adaptive Approach (EPAA) will probably provide only very limited capability against Russian long-range missiles, and then only if Russia chooses to fire these missiles on a particular trajectory. The SM (Standard Missile) interceptors due to be deployed will, on current plans, lack the velocities necessary to provide an effective capability against Russian ICBMs. The planned bases in Europe are designed to help to protect European NATO member states against a possible Iranian intermediate-range threat. Their locations are ill-suited, by contrast, to provide the US with protection against Russian long-range missiles being fired at its territory, which would take a trans-polar trajectory.[10]

As in the 1980s, however, it is the possibility of technological breakthroughs – the 'shadow of the future' – that is the main source of Russian concern at an operational level. Technology relating to strategic nuclear weapons and ballistic missiles is now relatively mature, is available to all the world's major powers, and is likely to remain a constant in their relations with each other. As the next section discusses, second-echelon nuclear capabilities – including NSNW arsenals and production capacities – are a focus of attention mainly because of their size, with little concern

---

[10]   For further technical discussion, see Dean A Wilkening, 'Does Missile Defence in Europe Threaten Russia?', *Survival* (Vol. 54, No. 1, February–March 2012), pp. 31–52.

over possible new qualitative developments. If these forces were the only elements in the equation, mutual vulnerability could be sustained with small nuclear forces just as well as with large ones.

By contrast, the possible development of new, game-changing military systems – such as strategic missile defences or strategically relevant conventional-strike capabilities – could threaten to erode this perception that mutual vulnerability is robust, and could thereby make Russia more reluctant to reduce to low numbers, and possibly persuade China to build up its own offensive arsenal. The UK and France already have 'minimum-deterrent' nuclear forces that are significantly larger than they would otherwise be because they felt the need to deploy MIRVs (multiple independently targetable re-entry vehicles) on their SLBMs in order to guarantee a capability for overcoming the limited missile defences then (and now) deployed round Moscow.[11]

Both countries could probably reduce the size of their strategic forces beyond currently planned levels were no such missile defences to be available. On a similar logic, but faced with the possibility of much more formidable US missile defences in the 2020s, it is not surprising that Russia is reluctant to reduce the size of its offensive forces without assurances in relation to US plans in this area.

Russia's specific concern appears to be as follows. In a future crisis or conventional war, the US might believe that it would be in its interests to launch a pre-emptive strike on Russia's nuclear forces (its ICBM fields, and bomber and submarine bases) along the lines of the Kaysen plan considered, but rejected, by President Kennedy back in 1961.[12] Russia's civilian casualties, and damage to its civil infrastructure, could be further reduced by mainly using US conventional forces for such an attack, which would have the additional advantage of minimising the risks of a globally catastrophic nuclear winter.[13]

In such a scenario, some Russian ballistic missiles would probably survive a first strike. Were Russia to try to launch a retaliatory nuclear strike against the US, however, the US would be able to use its (now greatly

[11] See Malcolm Chalmers, 'The United Kingdom: A Status Quo Nuclear Power?' and Camille Grand, 'France and Nuclear Stability at Low Numbers', in Malcolm Chalmers, Andrew Somerville and Andrea Berger (eds.), 'Small Nuclear Forces: Five Perspectives', RUSI Whitehall Report, 3–11, December 2011.
[12] See discussion above on p. 20.
[13] For further discussion of such 'splendid first-strike' scenarios, see David S McDonough, *Nuclear Superiority: The New 'Triad' and the Evolution of Nuclear Strategy*, Adelphi Paper 383 (Routledge for IISS, 2006). Also see Keir A Lieber and Daryl G Press, 'The Rise of U.S. Nuclear Primacy', *Foreign Affairs* (March/April 2006); Keir A Lieber and Daryl G Press, 'The Nukes We Need', *Foreign Affairs* (November/December 2009); Keir A Lieber and Daryl G Press, 'Obama's Nuclear Upgrade: The Case for Modernizing America's Nukes', *Foreign Affairs* (July/August, 2011).

enhanced) missile defence capabilities to shoot down what would now be a much-depleted attack. Russian leaders view US efforts to build strategic missile defence capabilities through the lens of such a scenario, and are concerned that the US is seeking to recreate the nuclear superiority which it last enjoyed at the beginning of the 1960s. Even if such a prospect does not mean that Russia will feel the need to increase its current forces, it may make it more difficult for it to reduce them to much lower levels. As such, it will continue to argue, as it has done consistently for decades, that strategic arms control needs to encompass both offensive and defensive capabilities.

Countering the Counter-Measures
So what can be done? Part of the answer will be found in countervailing military investments. In response to US investments in capabilities that could threaten its strategic forces, Russia is likely to continue to invest in means of protecting them. An increased emphasis on mobile, land-based missiles in its arsenal, for example, can provide some assurance against US conventional-strike capabilities, making it harder for the US to track their position reliably in a crisis without having much better reconnaissance capabilities.

It would not be enough, in countering such counter-measures, for the US to deploy systems that it has used with growing (but still patchy) effect against militarily weak states (such as Iraq and Libya), which are conveniently located near US air bases and carrier battlegroups. Instead, the US would have to be able to conduct such operations thousands of miles inside Russian territory, and against what are still quite formidable air defences. Similarly, while Russia's missile submarines may be especially vulnerable when in port, or when deployed nearby, this vulnerability could be reduced in response to an increased US threat. Its navy's possession of a significant arsenal of tactical nuclear weapons could also complicate US efforts to achieve maritime superiority in Russia's submarine 'bastions'.

If the US were to develop missile defence systems capable of threatening Russia, moreover, it could respond by enhancing its own capabilities for attacking those systems on land, in turn forcing the US to spend more on defending and duplicating those systems. An early, and very visible, taste of such a responsive tactic has been seen in Russian threats to deploy conventionally armed Iskander missiles in Kaliningrad, in order to pose a threat to US missile defence interceptors that are due to be based in Poland. Russia is also likely to be planning to hit fixed BMD-radar installations at an early stage of a conventional conflict, progressively degrading the overall coverage of the system. There are many other ways in which Russia (or indeed China) could cast doubt on the credibility of US missiles in the event of war, from direct attacks on US satellites (important for reconnaissance in both offensive and defensive operations) to various cyber-warfare possibilities. Importantly, Russia will continue to improve the ability of its ballistic missiles to penetrate enemy missile defences, for example through variable trajectories, short burn-times, stealth technologies and decoy warheads.

None of these options, up against the technological advantages of the US military machine, would be 100 per cent effective; but they would surely be effective enough to create sufficient confusion and uncertainty as to undermine the credibility of any US military leader seeking to convince a president that he or she can carry out a 'brilliant', and risk-free, first strike. More importantly, since few in the US leadership would harbour any such illusion, these counter-BMD capabilities could provide extra assurance to Russian leaders that their nuclear deterrent would not be undermined by US missile defence deployments.

Russia could complicate US first-strike calculations further, if it wished to do so, by continuing to invest in new missile defence capabilities of its own. To the extent that current plans for missile defence are seen as destabilising, this results not so much from the nature of defences in themselves, but in the fact that they could be disproportionately available to a single country (the US) that would also have many other military advantages.

If Russia (or China) were also to deploy its own missile defence systems, however, it could make it harder for the US to execute missile strikes reliably against its offensive forces. The mutual deployment of defensive systems might thus, at least initially, reinforce 'offence dominance' and mutual vulnerability. If such systems became progressively more capable, and offensive numbers declined further, the likely scale of damage caused by a retaliatory strike could begin to decline quite markedly, a development that is to be greatly welcomed. Nevertheless, the risk of unacceptable damage would remain inescapable, and would be significantly larger than in a world where only one country had significant defensive capabilities.

Russia, therefore, could find an 'answer' to US missile defence developments through military means alone. Doing so, however, would require it to spend more money on capabilities than it might otherwise want to; and the resultant competition would make it harder, politically if not operationally, for the US and Russia to press ahead with a programme of deep cuts in their offensive arsenals.

There would also be a danger that China might begin to emulate Russia's current nuclear posture, rather than providing a model of 'minimum deterrence' towards which Russia should move. Improved US missile defence capabilities could begin to undermine the faith that China's leaders have in the ability of its small force to provide an adequate retaliatory deterrent, and could spur it into an offensive build-up of its own (for example, through adding multiple warheads to its long-range missiles). In order to avoid such a development, any measures that the US takes to reassure Russia regarding its missile defence plans should also be designed to provide similar reassurance to China. For it would be impossible to achieve mutual restraint at low numbers, as defined in this paper, if China were – after decades of restraint – to decide that it had to increase the size of its strategic forces sharply in response to US BMD deployments.

Elements of Restraint
So what can be done to prevent a new offensive arms race driven by BMD concerns, which could possibly spread beyond the US and Russia to encompass China and other nuclear-armed states?

Efforts to develop a package of such measures are made more difficult by the widespread recognition that missile defence does have some utility, for example against accidental launches and against limited attacks from states such as North Korea and Iran, with which the major powers should not be expected to accept a state of mutual vulnerability. Missile defences are also likely to have a role against short- and medium-range missile threats, for example between Iran and its neighbours. The deployment of BMD for these purposes complicates efforts at achieving nuclear restraint at low numbers between the seven nuclear-armed states.

At the same time, efforts to distinguish between states which are and are not members of the 'club' will be helped by the disparity in material resources between the major powers, on the one hand, and the new challengers on the other. Six of the seven acknowledged nuclear-armed states possess a range of military advantages – geographical, financial and technological – that puts them in quite a different category from Iran and North Korea. Pakistan, with its vulnerable geography and limited military resources, falls somewhere in between the two categories. Mutual restraint at low numbers is likely to require India to accept a state of mutual vulnerability with its western neighbour; but it is hard to imagine that either the US or European NATO would be prepared to accept a similar state of affairs. Restraint in Pakistan's deployment of longer-range missiles, therefore, may be a condition for US and NATO restraint in deploying strategic missile defences.

If mutual restraint between the nuclear-armed states is to work, however, there will have to be an acceptance (explicit or implicit) that most of the key nuclear relationships between them will continue to be characterised by mutual vulnerability, even at low numbers. It is a legitimate and desirable objective of policy to seek to reduce the likely level of damage should nuclear war take place. However, states also need to accept that efforts to limit such damage through unilateral action can often be counterproductive. In particular, the US will need to make it clear – in practice as well as in principle – that it will not deploy BMD capabilities that would undermine the ability of Russia and China to preserve a minimum retaliatory capability against it. Similar self-restraint is likely to be necessary between India and China, as those states increasingly move towards a relationship of mutual nuclear vulnerability.

Co-operative Defence
It is still possible that co-operation between the US and Russia on European missile defence could play an important role. NATO Secretary-General Anders Fogh Rasmussen, along with many others, has argued that such co-operation could be a 'game-changer' in NATO-Russian relations, which, by its very existence, could convince both sides of the good intentions of the other; but the content of such co-operation would be crucial if such an ambitious objective is to be achieved.

Whatever 'joint' mechanisms are created, US-financed military assets – radars, interceptors, aircraft, ships – will remain under sole US control. Moreover, it would be unrealistic to expect that co-operation in this single area could, by itself, turn Russia into a full member of the European security community. Until such a wider peace has been created, therefore, the main purpose of co-operation, from a Russian point of view, will be to provide sufficient additional information about US capabilities as to alleviate concerns about the potential threat posed by new US BMD to their strategic forces. While highly desirable, therefore, BMD co-operation between the US, NATO and Russia would not remove the need for restraint in US deployments. As long as Russia believes it needs a secure second-strike nuclear capability against the US, it will be concerned – with or without co-operation – that the US should not be able to negate that capability by other means.

Any consideration of missile defence co-operation also needs to take the Chinese dimension into account. The US is already committed to enhancing co-operation on missile defence with Japan, India and South Korea. The long history of arms-control relations, however troubled, between the US and Russia – together with the structure provided by the NATO-Russia Council – also provides a framework within which BMD co-operation with Russia can be developed. However, success on this track would make it even more important for the US to reassure China that it had no wish to undermine the credibility of the latter's strategic nuclear force – which could also be the key to persuading China to sign up for nuclear restraint at low numbers.

Technology Unbound
With the US military leading the world in seeking new ways to take advantage of the multiple revolutions in technology that are now under

way (for example through improving cyber-warfare, nano-technology and distributed ISTAR capabilities), its Russian and Chinese counterparts will fear that such advances could, at some stage, lead to new breakthroughs in US BMD capabilities, to which they would have no effective response.

The US, in responding to such concerns, should be prepared to exhibit a greater degree of openness in explaining its plans and programmes to other major powers. Indeed, some progress in this regard is already being made, as part of NATO efforts to persuade Russia to sign up for co-operative missile defence. There are limits as to how far reassurance in relation to longer-term plans can help, given the speed at which new technologies can develop; but there is some comfort to be derived from the reality that, at least for now, Russia's concerns, as in the past, continue to overrun the actual capabilities of US BMD systems. The fourth phase of the EPAA, for example, involves the deployment of a new interceptor (the SM-3 Block IIB) whose performance has not yet been determined. Until the US knows what it can do, therefore, there is a limit as to what it can tell the Russians.

Defence Limits

Transparency measures with Russia and China – whether facilitated through co-operation or other means – would not contribute to confidence if they showed that the US was building an increasingly effective shield against their missiles. Unilateral restraint in the development and deployment of BMD – especially, but not only, by the US – could therefore also be needed as these technologies develop.

Restraint might, for example, involve restrictions on technical characteristics that distinguish those capabilities for theatre defence from those for defence against ICBMs. US experts argue that the SM interceptors due for deployment in Europe will not have sufficient velocity to pose a threat to Russia's ICBMs.[14] The US could make it clear that this will remain the case. It could also refrain from deploying missile defence radars and interceptors in locations – such as Iceland, the Baltic Sea and the Arctic Ocean – which are more optimal for intercepting Russia's ICBMs and SLBMs. Furthermore, it could unilaterally limit the number of missile defence interceptors that it deploys, and perhaps agree to Russian verification of these declarations.

Such measures, taken together, would provide some assurance that US BMD is only intended to counter the limited capabilities of states such as North Korea and (perhaps in the future) Iran. It would mark a revival, albeit on a more informal basis, of the arrangements in the ABM Treaty, which ultimately limited both countries to no more than 100 interceptors at

---

[14] Wilkening, 'Does Missile Defence in Europe Threaten Russia?', p. 49.

one site. Not least, the US should be ready to postpone the deployment and activation of new theatre missile-defence capabilities should the missile threat from Iran and North Korea develop less rapidly than currently feared. It should therefore make clear to Russia that one of the advantages of successful co-operation on the Iranian nuclear issue would be to reduce the need for further US missile defence deployments in Central Europe.

Securing Submarine Sanctuaries

Possibilities for mutual restraint in relation to maritime forces should also be explored. Both Russia and China are concerned that superior US capabilities for anti-submarine warfare could threaten the security of their ballistic missile submarines. It may, nevertheless, be possible to agree greater mutual restraint in monitoring activities that are seen as particularly threatening to the survivability of strategic missile submarines. Such concerns should be incorporated into thinking on future 'Air-Sea Battle' concepts being developed by the Pentagon on how to conduct a future war with China.[15] They might be developed as part of a process of enhanced confidence-building measures between the US and Chinese, and indeed US and Russian, navies.

Strategic Hedges against Strategic Defences

Last, but not least, nuclear restraint at low numbers – at least initially – is more likely to work if those countries that have the greatest concerns about missile defence are able to retain a capability for hedging against possible future US breakthroughs. New, and dramatically more effective, US capabilities could not be developed and deployed overnight; but they might emerge over a period of perhaps two to five years in the 2020s, for example in response to a deepening crisis in relations with Russia or China.

The possibility of retaining a 'hedge' strategic force against such a possibility has already been discussed. Even as the US and Russia cut their forces to levels well below the ceilings imposed by New START, they could retain the option of rebuilding those forces if necessary. Over time, they would have the option of institutionalising their reduced levels in a new treaty. Even without such a treaty, increased confidence that new BMD threats would not emerge could lead one or both countries to put their 'hedges' at progressively longer notices for redeployment. However, all of this will need consideration only at a later stage. For now, the important point is that mutual restraint within the existing New START agreement

---

[15] Greg Jaffe, 'U.S. Model for a Future War Fans Tension with China and Inside Pentagon', *Washington Post*, 1 August 2012.

could help soften the offence-defence linkage, which, at present, is one of the main obstacles to further mutual US-Russia reductions.

The Third Element: Restraint in the Second Echelon
The focus of the discussion so far has been on strategic systems covered by the New START agreement. Yet these form only part of the total nuclear arsenals of the US and Russia. While the US's New START declaration in April 2012 provided data on 1,737 deployed strategic warheads, the US's total operationally available arsenal amounts to around 5,000; and this latter total still excludes around 3,500 warheads that are intact but awaiting dismantlement.[16] Russia, for its part, announced a total of 1,492 deployed warheads under New START in April 2012, but is estimated to have a total of around 4,400 operationally available warheads, together with another 5,500 awaiting dismantlement.[17]

Most of the difference between the New START count and that for total operational warheads results from the large number of strategic missile warheads held in reserve, together with the undercounting of bomber-deployed warheads under New START. Russia is also estimated to have between 1,000 and 2,000 warheads (and perhaps more) available for use with non-strategic delivery systems (tactical aircraft and missiles, naval and air-space defence units), while the US is thought to have around 200 B-61 warheads deployed in Europe for use with NATO aircraft, together with more based in the US. Most of these weapons are held at relatively low states of readiness, but all could be made ready for use within a few weeks or months, and perhaps sooner, if necessary.

Furthermore, the US still possesses 14,000 plutonium pits, taken from previously dismantled weapons, a significant number of which could be used to reconstruct warheads if necessary. Although Russia probably has fewer available pits, it retains a large capability for producing new pits, estimated to be around 2,000 per year in a 2002 study.[18] Both states also possess large stocks of dual-use fissile material (highly enriched uranium and plutonium).

Both the US and Russia, therefore, possess a formidable panoply of what might be described as second-echelon nuclear capabilities, defined as capabilities that are not available for immediate military use, but which could contribute to such capability in future, given sufficient warning. While all these systems would have to be removed or placed under

---

[16] Hans M Kristensen and Robert S Norris, 'US Nuclear Forces, 2011', *Bulletin of the Atomic Scientists* (Vol. 67, No. 2, 2011), p. 66.
[17] Hans M Kristensen and Robert S Norris, 'Russian Nuclear Forces, 2012', *Bulletin of the Atomic Scientists* (Vol. 68, No. 2, 2012), p. 88.
[18] Oleg Bukharin, 'A Breakdown of Breakout: U.S. and Russian Warhead Production Capabilities', *Arms Control Today*, October 2002.

international control in order to achieve nuclear abolition, however, a lighter touch might be possible if the objective is instead to move towards mutual restraint at lower numbers of deployed warheads.

Indeed, at least in the initial stages of moving towards this goal, there could be some positive advantages (in terms of providing an assurance of second-strike capability) from not having too high a degree of certainty in relation to the number and (especially) location of second-echelon arsenals and stockpiles. The previous section of this paper pointed to the reassurance that a 'strategic hedge' could provide for states fearing a first strike at low numbers. A similar argument can be made in relation to second-echelon capabilities, which could provide a second, 'sub-strategic', hedge against surprise attack. Such a capability, hidden from the inspection (but not knowledge in broad terms) of potential adversaries, might be especially reassuring for countries – such as Russia or China – that are concerned about a disarming first strike, but do not face any realistic threat of a disarming invasion. For, while a 'long-fuse' hedge would not provide these states with capability for prompt retaliation in response to a disarming strike, it could provide them with the possibility of delayed retaliation. At the same time, because of their limited use in long-range, pre-emptive missions (with the partial exception of US ICBM and SLBM reserve warheads), possession of such capabilities is compatible with a programme for reducing New START-countable arsenals to much lower levels.

Including Operational Non-Strategic Weapons
Just as broad numerical parity with Russia is likely to be a political precondition for deep cuts in the US strategic arsenal, however, there will also be a strong political imperative for mutual reductions in non-strategic arsenals. NATO has called for reciprocal reductions in US and Russian NSNW in Europe; and the US Senate, in its letter of approval for the New START agreement, called for talks on the inclusion of these systems in future reduction agreements.

In discussing how best to incorporate second-echelon capabilities into a future restraint process, however, it is still useful to distinguish between systems that are more, or less, significant to the pursuit of stability at low overall numbers. This suggests a graduated set of policy prescriptions, with greater restraint and transparency in relation to non-strategic systems that are more readily available, and progressively less intrusiveness in relation to less-available capabilities. Such a structure not only focuses attention on those systems that are of greatest concern. It also avoids devoting scarce negotiating resources to the control of capabilities – such as plutonium pits and warheads awaiting dismantlement – that are of secondary concern for as long as both the US and Russia maintain large, active arsenals.

The first element of a package of second-echelon restraint, therefore, could be a set of measures designed to increase transparency, and promote restraint and reduction, in relation to operational delivery systems not currently covered by New START. These systems – missiles, aircraft and ships – continue to have a role in US and Russian nuclear arsenals, and are distinguished from those covered by New START mainly by their estimated range of operations. At least in relation to aircraft, however, their nominal range matters less than in the past, given the greater availability of refuelling capabilities. Such 'short-range' systems are a particular concern to the US's Asian and European allies, which view any nuclear system that can strike their own territory as inherently 'strategic'.

These systems could also become more important should the strategic arsenals of the US and Russia be reduced to only a few hundred apiece. In current NATO debates on the future of the 200 or so US nuclear weapons deployed in Europe, it is now conventional wisdom that these warheads have no operational role, and serve a purely political purpose. Yet it would be more accurate to state simply that they are surplus to operational requirements, given the massive size of the US's strategic arsenal. Were the size of the latter to be reduced to only 500, however, the 200 US warheads remaining in Europe would constitute a large proportion of total US capability. They might, with the benefit of better aircraft, refuelling and other support capabilities, be able to threaten a range of targets deep inside western Russia. They could, in short, regain a significant operational role.

A similar logic – that sharp declines in New START-counted arsenals could give increased significance to systems that are not so counted – applies to Russia's NSNW arsenal. Independent estimates suggest that Russia now possesses 450–750 non-strategic warheads deployed for use with land-based aircraft, 400–700 warheads deployed with naval forces, and 100–200 warheads for use with short-range, ground-based missiles. It is also thought to deploy 160–430 warheads for use with defensive (ABM and air defence) missiles.[19] Were New START arsenals to fall to fewer than 1,000 deployed warheads apiece, it would become increasingly important (politically and operationally) to focus arms-control and confidence-building efforts on these systems.

---

[19] Igor Sutyagin, 'Russian Non-Strategic Nuclear Potential: Developing a New Estimate', RUSI Occasional Paper (forthcoming, 2012); Hans M Kristensen, 'Non-Strategic Nuclear Weapons', Special Report No 3, Federation of American Scientists, May 2012, p. 53.

Platforms, not Warheads

The warheads for NSNW, like all nuclear weapons, are relatively small and easy to hide, especially if a state is willing to dispense with some of the associated security measures that are often the most visible marker of their presence. It probably makes sense, therefore, to focus arms-control and confidence-building efforts on the delivery systems involved in these capabilities, rather than on the warheads themselves. If this is done, the information exchange and inspection regimes needed to verify numbers of deployed NSNW delivery systems should be no harder than for the longer-range systems already covered under New START. It would require differentiation to be made between nuclear-equipped aircraft and those not so equipped; but this should not be a problem in principle, and is already a feature of some of the aircraft counted under New START.

Under such a transparency regime, for example, Russia might have to declare around 350 aircraft, forty-eight missiles and around 600 naval missiles and depth-charge launchers.[20] A further large number of air-defence and BMD missiles could be declared, though these might more appropriately be included in a separate missile-defence agreement. For its part, the US would declare what part of its non-strategic air-delivered arsenal remains nuclear-capable. The air forces of Germany, the Netherlands, Belgium and Italy, all of which retain aircraft equipped to carry US nuclear warheads, would also have to be covered in such an arrangement. Since all these countries have been at the forefront of efforts to promote greater NATO-Russia dialogue and transparency in this area, this should not be a problem. Both Italy and the Netherlands are currently planning to replace existing nuclear-capable aircraft with nuclear-capable F-35 aircraft, and a new transparency arrangement would also cover these systems. A process of further US-Russian mutual reductions might, however, convince NATO that such extensive nuclear-sharing arrangements are no longer necessary.[21]

Declaring Stockpiles

In addition, the US and Russia could start to introduce a further element of transparency by agreeing to make annual declarations of their total warhead stockpiles, including inactive second-echelon capabilities. The US has already made a single declaration to this effect, declassifying data on the size of its total stockpile, dating back to 1962. It has also announced

---

[20] *Ibid.*

[21] George Perkovich, Malcolm Chalmers, Steve Pifer, Paul Schulte and Jaclyn Tandler, 'Looking Beyond the Chicago Summit: Nuclear Weapons in Europe and the Future of NATO', Carnegie Endowment for International Peace, April 2012.

the number of warheads dismantled each year between 1994 and 2009. This announcement, made in 2010, showed that the total number of US warheads (active and inactive, but excluding those retired and awaiting dismantlement) was 5,113 in September 2009. This compared with 10,577 in September 2000, and 21,392 in September 1990.[22]

Other Nuclear-Weapon States have made similar announcements, with France stating that it had fewer than 300 warheads in its total stockpile in April 2008, and the UK declaring a total 'nuclear weapon stockpile ceiling' of 'not more than 225' in October 2010, due to be reduced to 'not more than 180 by the mid-2020s'.[23] In 2004, China stated that 'among the nuclear-weapons states, China has the smallest nuclear arsenal'. This statement has not been updated since the UK's most recent reduction, and is sometimes assumed to mean that China's 'arsenal' was, at least until 2004, smaller than that of the UK.[24]

All these declarations have some value as confidence-building measures; but this value is reduced by lack of definitional consistency (for example, the equivalence between a 'stockpile' and an 'arsenal') and by the unwillingness of any of the states concerned to make regular updates. Not least, Russia has so far made no such declaration, allowing a wide variety of estimates as to its total arsenal to flourish.

An initial step in this area could be for the Nuclear-Weapon States to agree on a glossary of terms for different types of warheads: distinguishing, for example (as the US does), between warheads that are active, inactive, in reserve and 'awaiting dismantlement'. Not all states have similar production and maintenance processes, so definitions may vary somewhat. The key, however, would be to increase confidence that unverified announcements had some relationship with reality 'on the ground', and were not simply the result of some creative wordplay. With this objective in mind, the five Nuclear-Weapon States announced in May 2012 that they had established a dedicated working group, to be led by China, which would 'continue working on an agreed glossary of definitions for key nuclear terms' with a view to 'establishing a firm

---

[22] US Department of Defense, 'Fact Sheet: Increasing Transparency in the U.S. Nuclear Weapons Stockpile', 3 May 2010, <http://www.defense.gov/news/ d20100503stockpile.pdf>, accessed 13 August 2012.
[23] HM Government, *Securing Britain in an Age of Uncertainty: The Strategic Defence and Security Review*, Cm 7948 (London: The Stationery Office, October 2010) pp. 38–39.
[24] Ministry of Foreign Affairs of the People's Republic of China, 'Fact Sheet: China: Nuclear Disarmament and Reduction', 27 April 2004, cited in Hans M Kristensen, 'Nuclear Arms Racing in the Post-Cold War Era: Who is the Smallest?', *FAS Strategic Security Blog*, 22 August 2007.

foundation for mutual confidence and further disarmament efforts', and further consider 'proposals for a standard reporting form.'[25]

States could also agree collectively to each make an announcement of the total size of their stockpile on an annual basis. Since the precedent of declaring this information on a one-off basis has already been set by the three NATO Nuclear-Weapon States, they may be able to take the lead on this, especially if they feel they have a good tale to tell. However, the focus in this regard should be to move away from transparency as a form of propaganda, and towards its institutionalisation as part of the wider arms-control furniture. China and, especially, Russia should be urged to do the same as part of the five-power nuclear dialogue.

Timing, Transparency and Broader Reductions
If Russia is interested in building confidence in this area, but still baulks at including its NSNW in the next step of formal arms control, it could take three steps to build confidence amongst other states in relation to these weapons. First, if, as some believe, it still has a larger total nuclear stockpile than the 5,000 now possessed by the US, it could move the number of warheads exceeding the US total to a 'retired' status, defined by the US as a weapon that is 'removed from its delivery platform, is not functional, and is not considered part of the nuclear stockpile. It is put in the queue for dismantlement.'[26] Secondly, having done this, it could announce the total size of its operational arsenal, using categories similar to those provided by the US in its unilateral statement in 2010. Thirdly, acting alongside the US, it could announce that it is prepared to draw down this total stockpile in coming years. Both countries would provide annual, publicly available reports on its progress in doing so.

Such a process, taken together with mutual reductions in New START-counted arsenals to around 750 apiece, could allow US and Russian total nuclear stockpiles to be reduced by around two-thirds: from current levels of around 5,000 warheads each to, say, around 1,500. This would still allow both countries to maintain significant arsenals of deployed non-strategic nuclear weapons (with Russia maintaining more of these systems) as well as of non-deployed strategic warheads (with the US more likely to maintain a numerical edge in this category).

This process would leave significant second-echelon capabilities unconstrained on both sides, including large US reserves of plutonium pits

---

[25] 'Statement by the People's Republic of China, France, the Russian Federation, the United Kingdom of Great Britain and Northern Ireland, and the United States of America to the 2012 Non-Proliferation Treaty Preparatory Committee, 3 May 2012', <http://www.un.org/disarmament/WMD/Nuclear/NPT2015/PrepCom2012/statements/20120503/P5_US_on_behabe.pdf>, accessed 13 August 2012.
[26] US Department of Defense, 'Fact Sheet: Increasing Transparency'.

made from disassembled warheads and Russia's greater capabilities for warhead production. There is room for debate as to whether, and how, these capabilities could be subject to greater mutual restraint. The argument of this paper, however, is that it would be better not to focus too much on them in the near term, instead accepting the existence of broad (albeit somewhat asymmetric) US-Russia equivalence and focusing restraint instead on those systems – predominantly warheads deployed on intercontinental ballistic missiles – that are most worrisome in terms of crisis stability. At a later stage in the reductions process, increased information exchange and verification in relation to these capabilities might play a useful role. Insofar as states continue to view these capabilities as having a particular role in their long-term 'hedging' strategies, however, it may be some time before such processes match those already in place for strategic systems.[27]

Focused Restraint and Appropriate Transparency
Together, the steps outlined above to promote confidence-building and transparency in relation to second-echelon capabilities would usefully support US and Russian moves towards mutual restraint at low numbers of deployed strategic weapons, while avoiding the pitfalls involved in an 'all-inclusive' approach. By continuing to focus attention on those systems that are potentially most destabilising (ballistic missiles), this approach can help to create the conditions in which other nuclear-armed states could be brought into the process. At the same time, it acknowledges that achieving and maintaining mutual restraint at low numbers will require a difficult balancing act: both carrying out deep reductions in numbers of nuclear weapons, while also avoiding the temptation to succumb to a 'numbers fetish' that would give much more weight to relative sizes of nuclear stockpiles than is justified by the requirements of finite deterrence doctrines.

Bringing in the Smaller Nuclear-Armed States
The nuclear forces of the US and Russia remain much larger in size, by a factor of at least ten, than those of any of the other nuclear-armed states. However, the more that the US and Russia could move towards mutual restraint at low numbers, the more that the smaller nuclear-armed states will come under pressure to join the process in some way.

---

[27] Acton places greater emphasis on curtailing these capabilities, but agrees that 'limiting production capacity should not be a goal for the next round of bilateral reductions, which is already overloaded with complex issues'. See James M Acton, 'Low Numbers: A Practical Path to Deep Reductions', Carnegie Endowment for International Peace, March 2011, pp. 24–27.

There is no realistic prospect that any of the other nuclear-armed states – even China – could overtake either the US or Russia in deployed warhead numbers during the first phase of post-New START reductions outlined above. Should the number of US and Russian deployed strategic warheads fall below 500 each, however, some might worry that China (which currently has fewer than 100 warheads in this category) could seek psychological advantage by subsequently announcing that it had 'leapfrogged' the two 'declining' superpowers and now had the world's largest nuclear arsenal. Such a move would not be consistent with China's restrained nuclear posture to date; nor would it have any operational significance – China could not use this numerical lead to put significant pressure on either the US or Russia. Concerns over such a possibility, however, still need to be taken seriously, given the wider uncertainties over the future direction of US-China strategic relations. Domestic support for deep cuts in both the US and Russia will depend, *inter alia*, on reassurance that China will not take advantage of their mutual restraint in an area of comparative advantage.

Avoiding New Parity Traps
In order to widen the process of nuclear restraint, one possibility would be to extend a New START-type system of numerical ceilings to other nuclear-armed states, perhaps starting with the NPT-recognised (and more longstanding) Nuclear-Weapon States (France, UK and China). Thus, for example, a group of American and Russian experts recently suggested that their two countries could reduce their total strategic arsenals to 1,000 warheads each, on 500 deployed launchers. They went on to argue, however, that:[28]

> It is hard to imagine, for example, that the United States and Russia would go below 1,000 total nuclear weapons if China was increasing its nuclear capacity... Further strides toward nuclear disarmament will be possible only if the other nuclear powers freeze their arsenals and join in the negotiation process to reduce their forces proportionately. For this stage, the United States and Russia could cut their arsenals to 500 nuclear warheads each in exchange for 50 per cent reductions by the other nuclear weapons countries.

However, it is likely that this particular suggestion would come up against strong opposition from the smaller nuclear-armed states. If, as some estimates suggest, China currently has a total arsenal of around 240 warheads, the American and Russian experts' proposal would require it to

---

[28] Bruce Blair, Victor Esin, Matthew McKinzie, Valery Yarynich, and Pavel Zolotarev, 'Smaller and Safer: A New Plan for Nuclear Postures', *Foreign Affairs* (Vol. 89, No. 5, 2010), pp. 9–16.

reduce this to 120, in order for the US and Russia to reduce to 500 each in turn.

A demand that the smaller nuclear-armed states accept institutionalised numerical inferiority in this way could have serious consequences. After decades in which the UK, France and China have been willing to size their nuclear forces on the basis of 'assured retaliation' criteria that have been unrelated to relative numerical strength, it would risk elevating the importance of numerical balances in the politics *vis-à-vis* their own nuclear forces, making it more difficult to involve them in the process of reducing national stockpiles. In particular, it would be seen as an attempt by the US and Russia to formalise their own nuclear superiority over all other nuclear-armed states, ultimately leading to a situation in which these two powers had adequate 'minimum-deterrent' forces, but others were obliged to have forces well below this level. China is now relatively relaxed about the numerical inequality between its own nuclear force and those of the US and Russia. If such a 'proportionate reduction' model were to be seriously pursued, it could bring the process of widening nuclear restraint to a halt at an early stage.

An alternative proposal would be to ask the smaller nuclear-armed states to adopt 'no increase' moratoria in relation to the size of their nuclear forces. An influential 1997 study of nuclear disarmament options by the US National Academy of Sciences (NAS), for example, proposed (in relation to France, the UK and China) that:[29]

> As long as these three countries pledge not to increase their nuclear forces and hold open the possibility of eventual reductions, the United States and Russia can reduce to a level of roughly 1,000 warheads without demanding reductions in their arsenals as a precondition.

The NAS study group went on to argue that the penultimate objective of the reductions process (prior to moving to complete nuclear disarmament) should be to reduce the arsenals of all five states to no more than 'roughly 300 nuclear weapons – of which at least 100 were secure, survivable, and deliverable', and suggested that this 'should be adequate to preserve the core (deterrent) function.' It made clear, moreover, that there should be no assumption that the US and Russia would automatically be entitled to retain more weapons than the other nuclear-armed states:[30]

> How soon the United States and Russia could move to a level of a few hundred warheads, and the other three declared nuclear powers to

---

[29] Committee on International Security and Arms Control, National Academy of Sciences, *The Future of U.S. Nuclear Weapons Policy* (Washington, DC: National Academy Press, 1997), p. 78.
[30] *Ibid.*, p. 83.

equal or lower levels (or perhaps zero), would depend more on political than technical factors...Russia's economic health, if not prosperity, would likewise be important to its willingness to proceed to a level that in nuclear terms would 'equalize it' with the United States, United Kingdom, and France but also with China.

The NAS was right to argue that deep cuts in the US and Russian arsenals would require some form of reassurance from the smaller nuclear-armed states as to their future plans. However, the timing and nature of these reassurances is likely to be critical. It is far from clear, in particular, why China should be expected to freeze the size of its arsenal at a level in the low hundreds as a condition for the US and Russia to reduce to 1,000 warheads each.

Reversibility and Reductions
Rather than insisting on early 'no increase' commitments from the smaller nuclear-armed states (or indeed from the US and Russia), it may therefore be more fruitful to focus on achieving rapid reductions, while allowing states some (suitably monitored) rearmament capability. As confidence grows in the credibility of reduced arsenals, 'hedge' capabilities could then be gradually reduced. This process could be accelerated if concerns over counter-measures (such as BMD) were to decline, or if wider security relationships were to improve. Agreement on deep cuts in front-line nuclear forces might, in itself, make some contribution to such an improvement.

While formal ceilings or permanent 'no increase' commitments for the smaller nuclear-armed states are either undesirable or unrealistic, however, a careful combination of restraint and transparency measures could reduce uncertainty on the current size and shape of their forces, and on their future plans, thereby removing one of the obstacles to US-Russia reductions to low numbers. Each of the five NPT-recognised nuclear-armed states is in a different geostrategic position, and at different stages of military and technological advancement; as such, a restraint and transparency package would have to take account of these differences. However, it is possible to outline a broad menu of possible measures from which choices could be made, largely mirroring those discussed above in relation to the US and Russia, and to be introduced in parallel.

First, and perhaps most important, the smaller nuclear-armed states should be asked to take on some of the information-exchange measures already adopted by the US and Russia as part of the New START agreement. Such a process would build confidence, in particular, in relation to small-power holdings of long-range missiles (ICBM and SLBM) and the warheads deployed on them. It would also initiate the involvement of the military establishments of France, China and the UK in a detailed strategic dialogue with their counterparts in the other Nuclear-Weapon States.[31] At this stage of the process, and given the proliferation sensitivities involved in sharing information relevant to weapon design, it would not be appropriate to include Non-Nuclear-Weapon States or international organisations in detailed information exchange and inspections. In line with their shared NPT obligations, however, the five states should publish the main outputs of these exchanges – such as missile and warhead numbers – as part of their regular reporting in the NPT review cycle. A parallel process of information exchange and publication could be initiated in relation to India and Pakistan, albeit outside an NPT framework.

There would be many issues to address in order to make such an arrangement work. For example, to make progress on an incremental basis, it may be preferable to start with unilateral declarations by the smaller states, to which each could add more detail as time went on, with a formal five-power (or seven-power) treaty as the culmination of the process, rather than the starting point. However, it would still be necessary to have agreement, from an early stage, on which systems should be included in the individual declarations.

Confidence in such an information exchange would be enhanced by agreement on a regime of mutual inspections, which would likely only be secured if it were to encompass (at a minimum) all five Nuclear-Weapon States. France and the UK would probably not be willing to enter into such a regime without China's participation, not least because it could be characterised as a NATO-Russia, rather than a global, arrangement. All three smaller Nuclear-Weapon States, in return for access to their own facilities, would also want to have inspection rights in relation to the strategic arsenals of Russia and the US. Concerns that inspections should enable technology transfer to a less technically advanced China might limit the extent of information exchanged, which may in turn impose further limits on the extension of an inspection regime to India and Pakistan. At the very least, therefore, it should not be assumed that inspection arrangements incorporating five or seven states would be as successful and in-depth as those for just two.

Including Medium-Range Systems
The seven nuclear-armed states should also consider extending the model of data exchange used in New START to include a wider range of delivery systems. The priority in this area would be medium-range and

---

[31] Detailed proposals along these lines are made in James M Acton, 'Low Numbers', pp. 56–61. Acton goes further than the proposal in this paper, however, by suggesting detailed information exchanges in relation to numbers and locations of all warheads, and not only those that are operationally deployed.

intermediate-range ballistic and cruise missiles, including those deployed at sea. Both the US and Russia are forbidden from possessing ground-based missiles of this range as a result of the INF Treaty. However, China's DF-3A, DF-4 and DF-21 missiles are believed to fall within the 500–5,500 km range covered by the treaty, as are France's M-45, India's Agni-I, II, III, IV and V missiles, and Pakistan's Babur cruise missile, Hatf and Shaheen ballistic missiles. In each of these cases, the missiles in question are an important part of their capability *vis-à-vis* potential opposing powers.

Other systems could be added to this data exchange, including all of the missiles (both ballistic and cruise) covered by the Missile Technology Control Regime (MTCR), whose Category 1 restrictions are focused on exports of missiles which can reach 300 km with a payload of 500 kg. Information exchange involving the smaller nuclear-armed states might also apply to shorter-range missile and aircraft nuclear delivery systems, in parallel with restraint and transparency measures required of the US and Russia. Importantly, such regimes – as with the New START and INF Treaties – would require an exchange of information on both conventionally and nuclear-armed missiles with these ranges. Conversely, a global INF Treaty (as proposed by France and Russia in 2008) would not be appropriate. The US and Russia were only able to agree to eliminating their medium- and intermediate-range missiles because of the large number of intercontinental missiles in their arsenals. China, India, Pakistan and Israel could not be expected to eliminate their own longest-range missiles, while getting nothing in return from the US, Russia and the UK.

Declaring Stockpiles

A further step, but perhaps the one that is least difficult in the short term, would be for all of the nuclear-armed states to announce the size of their total stockpiles on a regular basis, as the US, UK and France have already done. There could be some resistance to this in China in particular, especially from those within the government who want to preserve the maximum flexibility for converting fissile material into deployed warheads. However, the pressure to conform would surely grow should the US and Russia cut their arsenals further, especially once their deployed strategic weapons fell below 800 or so in number, at which point speculation in relation to China's future 'cross-over' capability would increase in the absence of transparency measures.

Widening Missile-Defence Restraint

The smaller nuclear-armed states could also contribute to restraint and transparency in relation to missile defences, although this would probably depend on whether the missile-defence capabilities of potential opponents (the US in the case of China, and Russia in the cases of France and the UK) could threaten the viability of their own second-strike capabilities. China and India, in particular, are also developing anti-missile and anti-satellite capabilities, which could be of concern to other smaller nuclear-armed states. A world in which all the nuclear-armed states deployed a mix of defensive and small offensive forces could, in principle, be relatively stable, because any state contemplating a disarming first strike could not be sure how many of its offensive missiles would reach their targets. Furthermore, anti-satellite weaponry could disrupt attempts to track and destroy mobile missiles, an important part of Russian and Chinese nuclear postures. In practice, however, deployment of strategic missile defences is likely to be highly asymmetric, with the most prosperous states – the US, followed by China and Russia – able to do much more in this area than, for example, Pakistan or Iran.

Incorporating China

If future multi-actor restraint is to be achieved, it is imperative that China's confidence in its second-strike capability should not be weakened in the process. Any US-Russian deal, perhaps as part of a broader plan to create a NATO 'from Vancouver to Vladivostok', that left China vulnerable in this way would risk driving it into reconsidering its current watchful, but relatively relaxed, relationship with Russia. Faced with such a perceived 'encirclement' (including the prospect of NATO-allied forces close to its northern frontier), China could respond by seeking to accelerate investment in its strategic offensive forces.

While the UK and France could probably be persuaded to accept most of the measures outlined above, as part of a programme adopted by the recognised Nuclear-Weapon States to fulfil their NPT responsibilities, they would be much more reluctant to go much further down this path if China were to refuse to join the process. A four-power restraint and transparency regime – excluding China – would risk being perceived as a NATO-Russia nuclear regime, which might also be seen as a step on the slippery slope towards accepting some form of nuclear parity between Russia and NATO as a whole, thereby legitimising Russian numerical advantage in relation to the US. More importantly, the UK and France would argue that they have already demonstrated themselves to be 'satisfied' nuclear states, with no intention of increasing the size or capabilities of their arsenals, and no need to do so. In contrast, there remains considerable uncertainty in relation to China's nuclear arsenal, as there is in relation to its defence build-up more generally.

Given the absence of any significant transparency in relation to its nuclear capabilities, China is often thought to be the biggest obstacle to five-power nuclear transparency. However, it should be noted that this assessment is being made at a time when both the US and Russia each maintain nuclear forces around twenty times larger than that of China, and when China is increasingly worried by possible developments in US missile-defence capabilities. Furthermore, in contrast to the UK and France, China has no significant allies (North Korea is more of a liability than an asset), yet it faces potential nuclear foes on at least three fronts.

In such circumstances, Chinese nuclear experts argue, China has a right to ask for concessions from others in return for greater transparency and restraint on its part; but in the absence of a convincing response, they suggest, it is not in China's interests to make unilateral concessions. A similar argument is made in relation to the CTBT. China has no intention of conducting further nuclear tests, and could gain significant credit as a responsible, disarmament-oriented power were it to ratify the treaty before the US (as France, Russia and the UK already have). However, its refusal to do so may in part reflect concern that, if and when the US Senate ratifies, it could attach conditions that would (in some unspecified way) be to China's disadvantage.[32]

If the US can reassure China that its BMD systems cannot pose a decisive threat to its second-strike capability, however, China's interests in a multi-actor process is likely to increase once the US and Russia reduce their own forces to fewer than 1,000 deployed warheads apiece. At this level, it would become increasingly less credible for the larger Nuclear-Weapon States to continue the reduction process without any assurance about China's capabilities and intentions. China would, in these circumstances, be faced with the option of taking a *quid pro quo* approach: to increase openness about its capabilities in return for further reductions in US and Russian arsenals. As a first stage, as outlined above, China could simply make a unilateral statement on the size of its total arsenal or stockpile; but, as US and Russian arsenals reduced further, it could then argue for a more formal five-power transparency regime, giving it the right to inspect the strategic forces of the US and Russia, and vice versa.

Many in China would be comfortable with this progression, which is consistent with its own longstanding doctrinal commitment to minimum nuclear deterrence and to No First Use. In the early years of its nuclear programme, China's leaders may have been constrained by their country's extreme poverty from investing in rapid growth in their nuclear capability. However, China has now emerged as the world's second-largest economy, projected to overtake the US in this regard in the 2020s. Its total military budget, variously estimated to be between $120 billion and $160 billion, is

---

[32] Author interviews with arms-control specialists, Beijing, March 2012.

growing rapidly.[33] Despite this growing wealth and power, however, it has not followed the US or Soviet Union in seeking to acquire a 'superpower' nuclear arsenal. There is no convincing evidence that it has acquired a tactical-nuclear-weapon capability, despite its continuing vulnerability to conventional defeat by the US Navy deployed along its shores. Its focus, instead, is on the slower (but more credible) option of building conventional capabilities – including more accurate, conventionally armed, ballistic missiles, as well as new submarines, aircraft and surface ships – in order to erode the US's superiority over time.

Nor has China sought a significant first-strike capability of the sort that also helped to explain the large arsenals created by the Cold War superpowers in the 1960s and 1970s.[34] Rather, like the UK and France, China appears to have structured its nuclear force around maintaining an assured retaliatory capability against any potential aggressor. This includes the possibility of retaliation against counterforce and counter-military targets.[35]

Unlike the UK and France, however, it has supplemented this doctrine with a commitment to never using its nuclear weapons first in any conflict.[36] In contrast to the Soviet Union's espousal of such a policy during the Cold War, moreover, it has created a force structure consistent with this declaratory policy. There is little evidence that China is seeking to develop a serious disarming counterforce capability, and its nuclear forces are currently kept at a low state of alert. Thus, Chinese experts make clear that in the event of a conventional invasion of its territory, China would resist with conventional means, if necessary using its vast territory to mount a prolonged resistance.

So what steps could China take, in return for US-Russian cuts in strategic forces, and US assurances on missile defence? It would need to be more transparent *vis-à-vis* the size of its current arsenal, both in terms of its deployed long- and intermediate-range missiles and its total stockpile. It would also need to provide greater assurance that it was not planning rapid growth in the size of this arsenal, for example by adding large numbers of multiple warheads to its existing long-range missiles.

Such restraint need not, and could not, be irreversible; but it would be desirable for China to make clear that restraint would be its settled policy unless new developments – such as dramatic increases in US missile

---

[33] *The Economist*, 'China's Military Rise', 7 April 2012.
[34] For a recent survey, see Christopher P Twomey, 'Chinese Strategic Cultures: Survey and Critique', SAIC, October 2006.
[35] Fravel and Medeiros, 'China's Search for Assured Retaliation: The Evolution of Chinese Nuclear Strategy and Force Structure', *International Security* (Vol. 35, No. 2, Fall 2010), p. 77.
[36] For further discussion, see Jeffrey G Lewis, *The Minimum Means of Reprisal: China's Search for Security in the Nuclear Age* (Boston: MIT Press, 2007).

defence systems – were to undermine the deterrent credibility of its nuclear force. Such a policy would not stop China's modernisation of its nuclear capability, replacing older systems just as the UK and France continue to do. However, it would undertake to discuss the content of these plans in advance, and reassure other nuclear-armed states that new systems would not provide additional capabilities.

In many ways, China should be an easier partner in a policy of restraint at low numbers than Russia, given that its trajectory of relative power – both political and military – remains in its favour. Even though its military capability will remain a fraction of that of the US for much longer than its national income, and despite lacking many of the US's wider strengths, current trends in defence investment will probably mean that the balance of overall military power continues to shift in China's direction, especially in relation to neighbouring states.

Such a benign picture (from China's perspective) could be upset greatly by a strategic shock, especially if it were to prompt China to embark on a rapid military build-up. Absent such an improbable shock, however, China's leaders are unlikely to suddenly abandon the policies of international passivity and low defence spending (as a proportion of GDP) that have served it well for the last three decades, instead preferring to focus on building up its economic and military strength, without sparking a confrontation with others.

Yet, over time, the growth of Chinese power could lead to increased tension, and even conflict, with the US and its allies. China already appears to be engaged in aggressive use of cyber capabilities in order to gain economic advantage, including access to advanced military technologies. So far, it has not sought to use its economic position in key developing regions (including the Middle East, sub-Saharan Africa and Latin America) to challenge US or European strategic relationships in these regions, as both the Soviet Union and China did during the Cold War; but it remains possible that it might do so in future, perhaps siding with resource-rich autocracies which share its interest in opposing US and European democratisation efforts. The US, for its part, seems set on a course of containing China's military power for as long as possible, hoping that a strategic *modus vivendi* can be developed, or that China's rapid economic development will falter as its population ages and its potential for capital-intensive growth is exhausted. As a recent major study of US-China relations, conducted by the Brookings Institution and Beijing University, concluded:[37]

> [T]he problem of lack of such trust is becoming more serious. Distrust is itself corrosive, producing attitudes and actions that themselves

---

[37] Kenneth Lieberthal and Wang Jisi, 'Addressing U.S.-China Strategic Distrust', John L Thornton Center at Brookings, Monograph Series No. 4, March 2012, p. vi.

contribute to greater distrust. Distrust itself makes it difficult for leaders on each side to be confident they understand the deep thinking among leaders on the other side regarding the future U.S.-China relationship.

If this trend were to continue, the process of seeking mutual nuclear restraint could not remain unaffected. In principle, the US could still push for deep cuts in nuclear arsenals as part of an effort to denuclearise international relations, and China could respond positively, recognising that (on this issue at least) the two countries had common interests and approaches. Nevertheless, sustained agreement on further steps in this direction is more likely if wider relations between the world's two most powerful states are improving, with common security efforts increasingly overshadowing areas of continuing tension and dispute.

However, despite the power of the US, Russia and China, achievement of restraint at low numbers cannot be a product of the five recognised Nuclear-Weapon States alone. The next section, therefore, considers how India and Pakistan might be brought into such an arrangement. The final section then examines how this system of mutual restraint could respond to the possible development of nuclear-weapons programmes in North Korea, Iran and other possible NPT defectors.

Incorporating India and Pakistan

The incorporation of India and Pakistan is necessary for a regime of nuclear restraint at low numbers to be sustainable. They are, however, quite different cases from the other small nuclear-armed states. Neither is recognised as a Nuclear-Weapon State in the NPT; but both are accepted as de facto nuclear-armed states, and no serious efforts (even rhetorical) have been made to reverse this status for many years. The debate on arms control in relation to these states, as a consequence, has turned to persuading them to take on the responsibilities that the NPT-recognised Nuclear-Weapon States already accept, including the pursuit of policies of restraint.

Yet the genesis and nature of the capabilities of India and Pakistan poses some unique challenges. The later development of their military nuclear programmes has helped to ensure that neither country has capabilities comparable even to those of the other three 'small' nuclear-armed states. Partly as a result, both states continue to build the size and quality of their nuclear arsenals at a pace that is no longer seen in the other nuclear-armed states.

India and Pakistan are estimated to have warhead stockpiles of 80–100 and around 100 respectively, less than half of China's estimated 240. However, recent estimates suggest that they are planning to produce enough fissile material to enable them to expand these arsenals quite rapidly over the next decade. India will need significantly more warheads to arm its emerging triad of delivery systems, which includes new, and longer-range, land-based missiles, together with submarine-launched ballistic and cruise missiles.[38] Pakistan is thought to be capable of producing new warheads at a rate of between seven and eighteen per year, which, if achieved, could see it overtaking the UK's numerical strength by 2020.[39]

Even if these numerical increases were to take place, however, they would not give these countries a nuclear capability comparable to those of France, the UK or China. Neither country is thought to have high-yield weapons, whereas all five NPT-recognised Nuclear-Weapon States have tested and deployed megaton-yield fusion weapons. The capability of India's and Pakistan's warheads may have been further constrained (though here evidence is fragmentary) by the very limited nature of their testing programmes, concentrated as they were in a short period in 1998. Although neither country has signed the CTBT, nor ruled out future tests, the political costs of such tests have, so far, prevented their flouting what are now fourteen-year-old moratoria.

Catching Up or Overtaking?
A similar pattern of lagged development exists in relation to delivery systems. Both states possess nuclear-capable bombers and missiles; however, neither has yet developed ballistic missiles with the intercontinental ranges that characterise the arsenals of the US, UK, Russia and China (France's long-range missile has a shorter range, but is submarine-based). Both countries continue with programmes designed to extend missile ranges, including India's Agni-V and VI, together with Pakistan's Shaheen-II (and possibly Shaheen-III). At the other end of the spectrum, both countries are also developing short-range weapons, including Pakistan's Hatf and Nasr and India's Prahaar.

The relatively short range of missiles possessed by India and Pakistan partly reflects technological constraints, but it is also geographically derived. Other actual or potential nuclear confrontations between major powers – the US-Russia and the US-China, China-India and Russia-Europe – are between countries whose centres of power are many thousands of miles from each other. Uniquely in the case of India and Pakistan, however, two nuclear-armed states have large population centres near a shared frontier. The vulnerability of Karachi and Lahore, Pakistan's two largest population centres, together with the vulnerability of its interior

---

[38] Hans M Kristensen and Robert S Norris, 'Indian Nuclear Forces, 2012', *Bulletin of the Atomic Scientists* (Vol. 68, No. 4, July/August 2012).
[39] Bruno Tertrais, 'Pakistan's Nuclear and WMD Programmes: Status, Evolution and Risks', *Non-Proliferation Papers* (No. 19, July 2012), p. 6.

lines of communication, has pushed it into increasing reliance on nuclear weapons to offset superior Indian conventional forces, leading it to invest in short-range nuclear weapons that could be used against invading forces. It has also meant that even 'strategic' missiles and bombers needed only a relatively limited range to reach the major population centres of the other state.

This is now changing. India is developing the Agni-V missile, which will have a range that allows it to target Chinese cities with key economic and political roles, such as Shanghai and Beijing. More importantly, India's policy-makers explicitly justify this development in terms of needing a credible retaliatory capability against China, matching the comparable capability that its rival already possesses. It may be several years before India is able to deploy significant numbers of Agni-V missiles, with one recent estimate suggesting that no more than two additional missiles will be deployed each year.[40] As such, it remains probable that India will still have fewer than 150 deployed nuclear weapons by the end of the decade, compared with more than 2,000 for both the US and Russia. Moreover, as Fravel and Narang argued in May 2012:[41]

> India is only now reaching the point of having an assured retaliation capability against China. Given China's superior capabilities, the eventual deployment of the Agni V will thus not weaken China's deterrent, even as it strengthens India's. China is unlikely to deploy more weapons in response, because its ability to survive a first strike by India remains robust.

Other commentators, in contrast, have expressed concerns that Asia could be on the verge of an arms race, with Pakistan racing to overtake India, India seeking to match Pakistan and catch up with China, and China unwilling to forego its role as Asia's largest nuclear power. James Acton, for example, argues that:[42]

> During the Cold War, nuclear reductions were essentially a U.S.-Russian bilateral issue. This will change in the not-too-distant future when the downward trajectory of the American and Russian arsenals risks colliding with the upward trajectory in China, India, and Pakistan.

It would not be politically practical to expect India and Pakistan to cap their nuclear arsenals at current levels. It also remains hard for the US and

---

[40] Pramit Pal Chaudhuri, cited in Shashank Joshi, 'The Arms Race Myth', *New York Times*, 23 April 2012.

[41] M Taylor Fravel and Vipin Narang, 'The Asian Arms Race That Wasn't', *Foreign Policy*, 8 May 2012.

[42] James M Acton, 'Bombs Away? Being Realistic about Deep Nuclear Reductions', *Washington Quarterly* (Vol. 35, No. 2, Spring 2012), p. 38.

Russia to demand that they do so, given their own much larger arsenals. Nevertheless, a slow growth in the numerical strength of India's and Pakistan's arsenals would still be compatible with achievement of nuclear restraint at low numbers. A move to Indian and Pakistani arsenals of 200 apiece by 2025, for example, would not be helpful to wider processes of nuclear disarmament; but it would not, in itself, prevent the US and Russia from carrying out deep reductions in their arsenals over the same period.

Will India Develop MIRV Systems?
Asian nuclear dynamics could pose a threat to achieving the objective of nuclear restraint at low numbers, however, in other ways. First, there is still a medium-term risk that India's attempt to build a credible deterrent in relation to China could overreach. When announcing the result of the Agni-V test in April 2012, the head of India's Defence and Research Development Organisation (DRDO) is reported to have said that India now plans to progress to the development of MIRV systems, a capability which China does not currently deploy.[43]

Such a scenario would involve considerable risks. As Narang and Clary suggest:[44]

> DRDO's pursuit of its own prestige may upset Asian strategic stability by triggering concerns in Beijing and Islamabad that India's nuclear posture is no longer one of 'assured retaliation' but one of 'nuclear superiority' that threatens the survivability of China's and Pakistan's nuclear forces...India finds itself in a strategically awkward position: advertising the development of a potentially destabilising cap that it does not yet possess and for which it has not yet articulated a clear rationale.

The views of the DRDO may not represent those of the Indian government as a whole.[45] What is clear, however, is that, if such a step were taken, it would pose a significant challenge to the maintenance of mutual nuclear restraint between India and China. A sharp increase in the size of India's long-range arsenal, constrained mainly by the supply of fissile material, could ultimately see it outstrip requirements for a minimum retaliatory capability in relation to China. Especially if combined with continuing development of India's missile defence capabilities, it might also be seen as

[43] *Deccan Chronicle*, 'India Eyes Agni-VI to Double Range', 20 April 2012.
[44] Vipin Narang and Christopher Clary, 'Capability without Strategy', *Indian Express*, 22 May 2012, <http://m.indianexpress.com/news/capability-without-strategy/952086/>, accessed 14 August 2012. The author thanks Shashank Joshi for this reference.
[45] Vipin Narang, 'Indian Nuclear Posture: Confusing Signals from DRDO', Institute for Defence Studies and Analysis Comment, 26 September 2011.

part of a move towards a disarming counterforce capability, designed to achieve some measure of nuclear superiority against its northern neighbour. China has, to date, been prepared to accept a degree of vulnerability to the US's counterforce capabilities; but it could be harder for China to accept such inferiority *vis-à-vis* India, especially if it had both a quantitative and qualitative dimension.

Is Pakistan Preparing to Fight a Nuclear War?

The second area of risk relates to short-range nuclear weapons, in which Pakistan, in particular, continues to invest additional resources. As in the case of the US, some capability in this area remains compatible with mutual restraint, provided that numbers remain small and its use essentially limited to a 'last-warning-shot' role. In addition to the risks of inadvertent use that such systems present, however, their increased deployment could also, in principle, lead Pakistan and India into an unchecked arms race at a 'tactical' level. Analysts and policy-makers in both countries are aware of such a risk; but an arms race in war-fighting capabilities still remains a possibility. Were it to take place, it would set Pakistan apart from the wider trend (evident even in Russia) for downgrading the role of tactical nuclear weapons.

Will India and Pakistan Bring Europe and the US Within Range?

Last, and potentially of greatest concern to other nuclear-armed states, are the risks that would be associated with further extension in the range of Indian and Pakistani ballistic missiles. Some Indian commentary has already argued that India has an 'intercontinental' capability because the Agni-V could hit Australia (if launched from the Andaman Islands), Europe (if fired from Kashmir or Delhi) or Africa (if fired from Gujarat).[46] Since the primary purpose of the new missile is to hold China's major cities at risk, such posturing for domestic purposes is unlikely to cause much concern in Paris, Nairobi or Perth. Were India to develop and deploy missiles with a range well in excess of that needed to reach China or Pakistan (or in excess of the range needed as a hedge against possible involvement in conflicts in the Gulf), this would be quite a different matter. Even if such a step were driven by technological prestige, it would risk being seen, not least by the US and European NATO members, as reflecting a growth in Indian 'hedging' against possible future disagreements with them.

The development of longer-range missiles by Pakistan (or indeed their deployment in Middle Eastern locations within range of Europe) would be of much greater concern, given the existing worries in relation to

---

[46] *Deccan Chronicle*, 'India Eyes Agni-VI to Double Range'.

that country. It would be seen as a dangerous symptom of strategic overreaching, and could provoke a fundamental reappraisal in relationships. Concerns over the political influence of jihadist extremism in Pakistan, together with concerns over the security of its nuclear arsenal, is widely thought to have led the US to develop extensive plans for securing this arsenal in the event of conflict.[47] Even if the Iranian missile threat can be contained, therefore, NATO plans for missile defence systems in Europe could continue to be justified by a possible threat from a rogue missile fired from Pakistan.

Satisfied by 2020?
The incorporation of India and Pakistan into a regime of restraint at low numbers by the end of this decade would need to address all three of these concerns. Most of all, it would require both states to demonstrate that, two decades after their 1998 tests, they had now become 'satisfied' nuclear-armed states. This would partly be a matter of declaratory policy, with both states making clear that, while system modernisation would continue, they would no longer need to seek enhancements in their nuclear capabilities. However, they could accompany this with specific steps designed to give credibility to this commitment. These could include continuing their moratoria on nuclear tests, even if US failure to ratify the CTBT continues to allow them to avoid a legally binding prohibition, and making clear that they had no requirement for adding multiple warheads to, or further extending the range of, their longer-range missiles.

India and Pakistan would, of course, expect concessions in return for such a package of restraint measures. Most of all, both would expect some formal recognition of their status as de facto nuclear-armed states, entitled to some sort of relationship with the five-power nuclear consultation mechanism that now reports to NPT review conferences. Thus, if the five Nuclear-Weapon States were to adopt joint transparency measures in relation to their delivery vehicles and warheads, this could provide India and Pakistan with an opportunity to do the same, providing assurance to others while cementing their positions as members of the nuclear 'club'.

Pakistan would also want to lift current Nuclear Suppliers Group restrictions on supplies to its civil nuclear programme, seen as particularly humiliating because of the more favourable treatment proffered to India. In return, Pakistan could be asked to remove its current veto of negotiations on a verifiable and legally binding cut-off in the production of fissile material for military purposes (in the form of the FMCT). Indeed,

---

[47] Jeffrey Goldberg and Marc Ambinder, 'The Ally from Hell', *The Atlantic*, December 2011.

agreement by Pakistan and India to such a treaty would be a powerful indicator that they had become 'satisfied' nuclear powers, and no longer sought further increases in their stockpiles of military fissile material. Even if it proves impossible to reach consensus on such a treaty, India and Pakistan could announce moratoria on fissile material production, similar to those announced for nuclear tests, without giving up the right to re-start such production in future. This would bring them into line with the practices already adopted by the other Nuclear-Weapon States, and would be compatible with the 'focused restraint and appropriate transparency' concept outlined in this paper.

India, China and Pakistan
India and China are strong candidates to become 'satisfied' nuclear-armed states, confident in the credibility of their second-strike retaliatory capabilities. The risk of war between the two countries remains a real concern, most recently demonstrated by India's reinforcement of its ground and air forces near its eastern border with China. However, neither need give much credence to the possibility of significant conventional threats from the other to their very existence as states, and even if war were to take place between the two states, there would be strong incentives on both sides to limit the conflict, as happened during the month-long conflict of October 1962. India's acquisition of a secure retaliatory capability against China should, in this context, further reduce concerns that conventional conflict between the two would escalate.

Even if India and China are on course to become 'satisfied' nuclear-armed states, however, Pakistan's progression will be more difficult. Due to its relative weakness in conventional military power, together with its lack of geographic depth in the event of war with India, Pakistan continues to position nuclear weapons more centrally in its national security posture than any of the other nuclear-armed states. While these states should try to bring Pakistan into a regime of mutual restraint, therefore, they may also need to consider how they should act if Pakistan were to stand alone.

In particular, the other nuclear-armed states may need to be willing to make it clear to Pakistan that there would be real costs involved in standing aside from a wider international effort aimed at restraint. For instance, of the nuclear-armed states, Pakistan spends the least, by a large margin, on conventional military spending, with a 2011 defence budget estimated at only $6 billion – a fraction of the $50 billion allocated by India, the more than $60 billion by each of France and the UK, and the more than $70 billion by Russia.[48] While this disparity helps to explain why Pakistan feels especially reliant on nuclear weapons for its security, it also leaves

---

[48] SIPRI, Military Expenditure Database, 2012.

Pakistan ultimately more dependent on others for that security, and in time may make it more aware of the costs of strategic overreach.

Israel

Of all the states that now possess nuclear weapons, Israel is by far the smallest, in terms of both population and geographical area. Although it has never acknowledged that it has nuclear weapons, it is estimated to have an arsenal of between 100 and 200 warheads. It is thought to have a triad of delivery systems, including aircraft, land-based ballistic missiles and diesel-electric submarines (the latter provided by Germany).[49] It is now one of only three countries (with India and Pakistan) that have not signed the NPT.

Since its initial creation in the late 1960s, Israel's nuclear arsenal has been a focus of complaints from neighbouring states, which point to it as an indication of US and European double-standards on non-proliferation. Successive attempts by other countries in the region to acquire nuclear-weapon capabilities – by, successively, Iraq, Libya, Syria and now Iran – have been legitimised (and may have been partially driven) by the existence of a potentially hostile state, armed with its own nuclear weapons, in their immediate neighbourhood.[50]

Israel's nuclear programme is a focus of strong criticism from Turkey, whose willingness to support its NATO allies on Iran has, at times, been diluted by the stark contrast in treatment between it and a country that has already acquired such weapons outside of the NPT regime. Successive NPT conferences have seen strong concerns over Israel's programme expressed, with other non-aligned countries lining up with Egypt and other Arab states in their criticism. It remains a difficult part of the NPT 'package' to sell internationally, contributing to a perception that the treaty disproportionately benefits the US and its allies.

These diplomatic tensions, for now, are being managed through a common international commitment to a Middle Eastern zone free of weapons of mass destruction, most recently reaffirmed at the 2010 NPT review conference. Yet, even if the initial meeting does take place as scheduled in late 2012 with participation from both Israel and Iran, progress on the substance of the zone is difficult to imagine until there is a wider political reconciliation between Iran and its neighbours. If anything, regional political trends point to increasing turmoil. The wave of

---

[49] For a compendium of the different estimates that have been made, see Avner Cohen, *The Worst Kept Secret: Israel's Bargain with the Bomb* (New York: Columbia University Press, 2010), pp. xxvi–xxvii.

[50] Amatzia Baram, 'Deterrence Lessons from Iraq: Rationality is Not the Only Key to Containment', *Foreign Affairs* (July/August 2012).

successive uprisings in Arab states has not yet run its course, the political future of Israel's occupied Palestinian territories seems further from resolution than ever, and Iran's anti-Zionist rhetoric remains intransigent and hostile.

Yet Israel's nuclear arsenal does not figure prominently in discussions of future multi-actor arms control. This reflects, in part, the opacity surrounding its programme, which makes it more difficult to make comparisons between its capabilities and doctrine and those of other nuclear-armed states. However, it also results from the fact that, insofar as these exist at all, Israel's primary deterrent relationships have been with non-nuclear states – the Arab states and Iran – that have threatened it with attack or invasion.

Importantly, in this respect, Israel has managed to avoid any discussion of possible deterrent relationships with the other seven nuclear-armed states. None of these states, as a result, would be likely to require Israeli reciprocation in order to move towards greater mutual nuclear restraint at low numbers. Where a wider process of restraint might make a difference, however, is in relation to global instruments other than the NPT. Israel has signed the CTBT (and it would be likely to ratify the treaty if the US were to do so), and hosts two auxiliary seismic monitoring stations and a radionuclide laboratory. It is also unlikely to have problems with an FMCT if other nuclear-capable states (especially in its neighbourhood) were to sign up. Indeed, given the relatively mature status of its programme, it would probably feel that such a treaty was to its benefit.

A process of further regional nuclearisation – led by Iran – could, however, lead to greater involvement of extra-regional nuclear-armed states. There is already much discussion as to a possible role for US extended nuclear deterrence for Gulf Cooperation Council states in the event of Iran acquiring a bomb. More speculatively, Iranian nuclearisation could lead to a growing role for Pakistan as a supplier of nuclear protection or weapons to Saudi Arabia. The implications of such a development for Israel, if it were to happen, could be profound. Pakistan is the only one of the seven nuclear-armed states that does not have diplomatic relations with Israel (North Korea is in the same position), and Israel may assume, as a result, that it could be a potential nuclear adversary. If such a relationship were to begin to develop, however, it could have far-reaching consequences for nuclear doctrine and targeting, as well as declaratory policy, in both states. The more that Israel becomes drawn into deterrent relationships with a nuclear-armed state in this way, however, the more difficult it may find it to maintain its policy of opacity.

Defecting from the NPT

The nuclear programmes of the three NPT non-signatories (India, Pakistan and Israel) have now been accepted as a fact of life by the five NPT Nuclear-Weapon States, albeit reluctantly. Those states that have entered the NPT as Non-Nuclear-Weapon States, and then sought to develop programmes covertly, have often experienced much harsher treatment. This reflects a strong desire to avoid the dangerous precedents that would be involved in allowing states to use the NPT as a means of legitimising civil nuclear programmes, under the cover of which military projects are then pursued.

There have been several states in this category in the past, and there could be many more in future. At the time of writing, however, the spotlight of concern is focused on two states: North Korea, which left the NPT in 2003, has since conducted two nuclear tests, and openly proclaims that it has nuclear weapons (albeit probably only a handful); and Iran, which remains in the NPT, strongly asserts the peaceful nature of its nuclear activities, but is widely suspected of seeking to build a military capability.

The nuclear and missile programmes of North Korea and Iran have already become key accelerants for US missile defence efforts in Asia and Europe respectively, with potentially serious consequences for US-China and US-Russia nuclear relationships. If they consolidate and develop, moreover, both risk triggering proliferation cascades: from North Korea to South Korea and perhaps even Japan; and from Iran to Saudi Arabia and perhaps in time to Egypt.

Yet both states are seeking to acquire nuclear capabilities from a position of strategic and economic weakness. The international community, as a result, retains an array of instruments – financial incentives, economic sanctions, potentially even conventional military action – that it can use to prevent, contain and possibly reverse their efforts. Even if Iran were to successfully explode a nuclear device, as India and Pakistan did in 1998, the rest of the world (and the US in particular) would be unlikely to accept this as a *fait accompli*. Rather, as with North Korea, international pressure on Iran would almost certainly intensify, not recede, if it presses ahead with nuclearisation. Indeed, the very intensity of pressure being applied to the two states highlights the continuing importance that other states assign to upholding NPT norms.

Provided that proliferation can be confined, at worst, to these two 'outlaw' states, it need not have a significant effect on efforts to build mutual restraint amongst the existing nuclear-armed states. Even if, for example, the US were to be involved in a future militarised crisis with North Korea, conventional and missile defence forces would play the primary roles in deterring, and if necessary blunting, North Korean nuclear use. In the event of such use, the US's primary military response would probably be directed against those responsible for such a decision, seeking as far as possible to exclude civilian populations from any effects. Even so, there might also be deterrent and reassurance roles for the US's own nuclear weapons, most notably through holding open the possibility of a retaliatory strike. Against a small country such as North Korea (or Iran), however, such a strike would only require a small fraction of the force of the several hundred warheads that the US would retain under the mutual restraint scenarios outlined in this paper.

The longer that 'break-out' by North Korea or Iran persists, however, the greater the risk that their status as de facto nuclear-armed states would become accepted. One of the major powers, for example, might break ranks and seek economic or political advantage by breaching international sanctions. Internal regime change could take place, opening the possibility of political reconciliation with the US in return for acceptance of nuclear status. Saudi Arabia could itself nuclearise, making it more difficult to maintain a sanctions regime designed to hold the line at Iran.

Beyond the Middle East, there is a wider group of technologically advanced countries which maintain a significant capability for 'break-out' from their current non-nuclear status. Japan is perhaps the primary member of this group, and figures prominently in China's concerns in relation to the nuclear balance in East Asia.[51] There continues to be an active debate in Brazil about the strategic utility of nuclear capabilities, together with resentment towards the double standards implicit in both the NPT itself and the US-India nuclear deal.[52] Nor can one rule out the possibility that other technologically advanced states – such as Argentina, South Africa and South Korea – might also resuscitate past military programmes in the event of an NPT breakdown or the emergence of new national security threats.

As more countries acquired nuclear weapons, and the NPT lost its normative status or even collapsed altogether, proliferation could accelerate further. Current export controls, and other measures designed to control nuclear-entry costs, could fall away, encouraging more states to cross the nuclear threshold.

In such a world, concepts of finite deterrence and mutual restraint at low numbers would continue to be relevant. The risks of actual nuclear conflict would be greater in a world of twenty nuclear-armed states than in one of eight, not least because of the likely identities of the additional

---

[51] Andrea Berger and Malcolm Chalmers (eds.), 'Forging UK-China Consensus on a Strengthened NPT Regime', RUSI Occasional Paper, 2012, especially pp. 17–18, 48.

[52] Sarah Diehl and Eduardo Fujii, 'Brazil's New National Defense Strategy Calls for Strategic Nuclear Developments', Nuclear Threat Initiative Issue Brief, 30 October 2009.

twelve, so efforts to limit the damage from nuclear war would become even more important than ever. Yet, in such a scenario, it would also become more difficult to persuade the US and Russia to continue to reduce their nuclear arsenals, or to persuade India, Pakistan and China not to increase their more modest capabilities. The prospects for achieving nuclear restraint amongst existing nuclear-armed states at low numbers, therefore, may depend in large measure on whether other nuclear programmes (such as those of North Korea and Iran) can be contained or reversed.

V. CONCLUSIONS

Getting the sequencing right will be key to the success of the next stages of nuclear arms reductions. A process that moves too quickly to seeking a new legally binding agreement on total stockpiles, rather than using the existing New START framework to push forward with deep cuts in deployed forces, could end up mired in interminable discussions of how to define and verify what is, and is not, a 'warhead'. Premature demands to place binding limits on the arsenals of the smaller nuclear-armed states will have little purchase as long as the US and Russia maintain forces that are some fifteen to twenty times as large as those of China and France, and perhaps fifty times as large as those of India and Pakistan. Even if the political will to make progress on nuclear disarmament were to exist, it might not be realised in practice.

A more appropriate sequencing, by contrast, is likely to involve a willingness to proceed incrementally, focusing on restraining those systems that are of greatest concern, and developing transparency measures appropriate to the task of supporting this restraint. Given the disparity in capabilities that still exists between the large and small nuclear-armed states, the first priority remains a further reduction in the deployed strategic forces of the US and Russia. Using the New START framework, it should be feasible to imagine a verifiable halving of such forces before the end of this decade (to 750 deployed warheads apiece), opening the way to further bilateral reductions in subsequent years. In parallel, it would be helpful – though not, it should be emphasised, essential – for the two large nuclear states to increase reciprocal transparency in relation to other (second-echelon) nuclear forces, including short-range missiles, nuclear-capable aircraft, warheads in storage and fissile material stockpiles. Progress on these two fronts should be seen as reinforcing but not mutually dependent.

Even if the US and Russia were to reduce their deployed strategic arsenals by 50 per cent by 2020, and accompany this with a 50 per cent reduction in warhead stockpiles, they would still have nuclear forces that were qualitatively more capable than those of the smaller nuclear-armed states, as well as being between five and ten times as large. Neither could reasonably expect, therefore, that this initial phase of reductions should be dependent on specific restraint measures from the five smaller states. Indeed, it is likely, at least in the cases of India and Pakistan, that some continuing build-up in small nuclear forces could be taking place.

Yet it is not too early to begin thinking about what the next stage of mutual nuclear restraint might look like, and what its objective should be. The objective most likely to command wide support would be a joint commitment to nuclear restraint at low numbers, a scenario in which all the nuclear-armed states feel comfortable that they can meet their nuclear deterrent requirements with total warhead arsenals numbering in the low hundreds. The UK and France are already 'satisfied' nuclear-armed states in this regard, with no perceived requirement or plan to increase their capability above this level; but more would have to be done to persuade China, India and Pakistan to move into this category, and to convince others that they had done so.[1]

The requirements for reaching this objective of mutual 'satisfaction' with nuclear capabilities are well defined in the arms-control literature. On the one hand, states need to believe that their forces (together with those of their potential opponents) provide an adequate level of 'crisis stability', so that incentives to strike first are minimised by the existence of credible second-strike, retaliatory capabilities. If such stability exists, the circumstances in which the use of nuclear weapons can be credibly threatened are sharply circumscribed, thereby allowing states to be satisfied with arsenals numbering in the low hundreds rather than in the thousands. The more expansive roles that justified the large superpower arsenals of the Cold War, and in particular their possible use in war-fighting and disarming counterforce attacks, are much less credible than they were in the past. The role of nuclear weapons, instead, is increasingly confined to deterring their use by others and possibly (for some states at least) to deter invasion of national territory by superior enemy armies. The US's nuclear forces also have the additional role of seeking to deter nuclear and invasion threats against its closest allies.

Nuclear restraint at low numbers also requires a degree of 'arms-race stability', so that risks to crisis stability as a result of new military capabilities are relatively limited and manageable. Thus, for example, Russian and Chinese support for mutual restraint at low numbers will be more likely if the US deployment of missile defences does not develop in ways that undermine their abilities to maintain a credible retaliatory capability.

---

[1] For a more detailed discussion of the five 'small' nuclear forces, and in particular their categorisation as 'satisfied', 'restrained' or 'embattled', see Malcolm Chalmers, 'Introduction and Overview', in Malcolm Chalmers, Andrew Somerville and Andrea Berger (eds.), 'Small Nuclear Forces: Five Perspectives', RUSI Whitehall Report, 3–11, December 2011.

The onward march of technology, however, means that arms-race stability can never be absolute. In areas as diverse as robotics, cyber-warfare and anti-submarine warfare, new technological advances (both civil and military) could threaten to undermine the credibility of minimum-deterrent forces. Mutual nuclear restraint cannot prevent nuclear-armed states from modernising their forces in ways that minimise their exposure to new risks arising from technological change; but it can provide mechanisms through which these states could reassure each other so that such modernisation did not itself become a source of instability.

Attempts to maintain arms-race stability are complicated by the large disparities that exist in conventional long-range strike and strategic defences, and in the potential 'break-out' options that these might allow. It is not practical, and probably not even desirable, to limit these disparities through formal arms control.

Especially at the earlier stages of a mutual restraint process, therefore, states (especially those which are conventionally weaker) are likely to want to preserve the ability to 'hedge' against future uncertainties of this sort, for example by rebuilding demobilised forces. Such concerns relating to strategic forces, for example, may strengthen the case for focusing on achieving verifiable reduction in deployed strategic warheads, while allowing for less intrusive transparency measures in relation to non-deployed warheads and fissile material.

Moving towards mutual nuclear restraint at low numbers is plausible, most of all, because it goes with the grain of thinking in most of the nuclear-armed states. Whatever the ambiguities in the declaratory policies of most Nuclear-Weapon States, the absence of any operational use of nuclear weapons since 1945 speaks for itself. Despite multiple conflicts since that time, including several inter-state conflicts involving nuclear-armed states, this tradition of non-use has cemented the perception that nuclear weapons could only be used in a very narrow range of scenarios, the least incredible of which would be in retaliation against a nuclear attack. This tradition, driven most of all by lack of operational utility, has been further reinforced by normative and legal constraints.

It is not possible to make a definitive judgement as to whether nuclear weapons have played an indispensable role in the prevention of war between the major powers since the 1950s. Insofar as such a total-war-deterring effect does exist, however, it probably relates more to the knowledge that such weapons exist and could be used than to any specific configuration of arsenals. Such 'existential deterrence', therefore, may be compatible with the weapons' continuing marginalisation as an active ingredient in the practice of international power politics. At least for the major powers, therefore, the stage could be set for a nuclear demobilisation, in which some minimum capability is retained as a hedge against an uncertain future, but in which the expectation of any actual use continues to be very low indeed.

Going with the NPT Grain

A trend toward nuclear demobilisation amongst the nuclear-armed states would be widely welcomed by other states. Most of the world's Non-Nuclear-Weapon States view the issue of nuclear disarmament through the prism of the regime of mutual obligations established through the NPT. When the treaty entered into force in 1970, five of today's nuclear-armed states had already tested, and two others (Israel and India) were capable, or almost capable, of doing so. Since that time, however, only one state (Pakistan, which launched its programme in 1972, following the loss of Bangladesh to Indian invasion) has successfully acquired a deliverable nuclear arsenal. Many other states (notably in Europe) had already decided to forego a nuclear option before the NPT was agreed; but the treaty helped to consolidate this decision, with memories of past weapons programmes fading quickly from political consciousness.

Even more importantly, many other states gave up nuclear-weapons programmes in subsequent decades. They may have done so in part because of the growing strength of international non-proliferation norms, symbolised by the NPT. Yet they also did so because of the growing commitment of the US and its allies to act to curb proliferation, a task in which they were greatly assisted by the existence of the NPT. Several key states have also abandoned weaponisation programmes after years of effort, whether through regional agreement (such as Brazil and Argentina), as a result of geopolitical change (South Africa), in the wake of state break-up (Ukraine, Kazakhstan and Belarus) or in response to international military pressure and related inspections regimes (Libya and Iraq). It remains to be seen whether North Korea or Iran could succeed where others have given up. After devoting a large part of its national resources to do so, North Korea has been able to produce a handful of nuclear devices. It has not, however, so far shown a capability to produce a deliverable weapon.

Iran is also widely thought to be seeking some level of nuclear-weapons capability, but growing international pressure may yet persuade its leaders that it will be more secure if it does not cross the threshold into full nuclear-weapons capability.

Even as efforts continue to build on this relative success, however, expectations that the Nuclear-Weapon States need to do more to fulfil their side of the NPT bargain have grown and strengthened. It is important not to be unduly legalistic when discussing the exact nature of these obligations. The wording of Article VI of the NPT, for example, has at times been interpreted to mean that complete nuclear disarmament is only required in circumstances of 'General and Complete Disarmament', effectively making the commitment devoid of real meaning. Despite its vague wording on key points, however, understanding of what the NPT requires has evolved and strengthened over time, most particularly as a result of the conditions for the treaty's indefinite extension that were agreed in 1995.

For Non-Nuclear-Weapon States, the burden of proof of compliance has increasingly shifted towards states of concern, with the Additional Protocol obliging its signatories to accept a much more intrusive inspection regime, and the UN Security Council ordering NPT signatories (such as Iran) to take additional measures in relation to their enrichment programmes which, for other states, are seen as being entirely within the provisions of the treaty.

In the two decades that followed the Cold War, moreover, the establishment of regular five-yearly reviews of the NPT has begun to provide some institutionalisation, albeit modest, of pressure on the Nuclear-Weapon States. This pattern began with the 1995 Review and Extension Conference, which extended the treaty indefinitely, and was continued at the 2000 conference, at which the Nuclear-Weapon States agreed to take thirteen concrete steps towards fulfilling their Article VI commitments. No consensus was possible at the 2005 conference, but agreement did prove possible at the 2010 conference, largely because the US (and other Nuclear-Weapon States) had taken concrete measures – the New START treaty and the agreement to hold a Middle Eastern weapons-of-mass-destruction conference – that demonstrated continuing progress on the disarmament agenda.

The NPT, therefore, should be seen more as a frame of reference – or 'framework treaty' – than as a detailed and prescriptive agreement comparable to the New START or INF Treaties. In this way, it has helped to underpin, and provide international legitimacy to, the progressive development of norms of responsible behaviour for both Nuclear- and Non-Nuclear-Weapon States. There is, as a result of this process, a broad recognition that the Nuclear-Weapon States have a collective responsibility to pursue nuclear disarmament in good faith.

Not with a Bang, but a Whimper

While this paper has focused on the feasibility of moving towards nuclear restraint at low numbers for the seven acknowledged nuclear-armed states, it does so in the context of a wider, and vigorous, debate about the goal of complete nuclear disarmament. Ever since the dawn of the nuclear age, influential leaders have urged states to agree to move towards this goal. Support for this objective has been given fresh momentum, in recent years, by the strong support it has achieved from President Obama of the US.

Supporters of nuclear abolition accept that it cannot be achieved overnight, and that a series of intermediate steps will be needed before states are ready to take the final decisions necessary to achieve it. Moving to nuclear restraint at low numbers, therefore, can be viewed as part of this process, reducing the roles and numbers of nuclear weapons, and thereby making the 'final step' towards abolition rather less radical than it currently appears. Not least, the process of aiming to achieve nuclear restraint at low numbers should help focus minds on the mutual interest that the nuclear-armed states have in addressing each other's concerns about the vulnerability of their forces to disarming first strikes by each other, as well as to armed aggression more generally. Nuclear restraint, in this respect, is part of a wider process of finding co-operative solutions to the security dilemmas which these states face, and avoiding wars that none of them wants.

The feasibility and desirability of moving to nuclear abolition would, however, depend on a number of additional conditions being met, over and above those needed for nuclear restraint. In one model of abolition, for example, it would be necessary to create an intrusive international regime that places all nuclear activities (civil and military) under effective international control, thereby making it possible to ensure that no state could acquire the ability to produce or hold nuclear weapons. The inspections necessary for nuclear restraint at low numbers could provide the basis for these, in practical and normative terms.[2]

In order for civil nuclear activities to be economically viable, however, they will still have to be widely dispersed, including on the territories of states (such as Russia, China and the US) which have had nuclear weapons in the past, and would retain knowledge of how to recreate them in future. As long as these states still feared that they might one day face the possibility of large-scale war with each other, they would each want to make some preparations against the possibility that the others might seize the nuclear materials on their own territory, and then rush to rebuild weapons capabilities. There would be a danger, as a result, that complete nuclear disarmament could heighten, rather than reduce, the salience of nuclear weapons in a future international crisis. Rather than keeping nuclear weapons in the background for as long as possible (as could be done under a restraint regime), decision-makers might feel obliged to rebuild nuclear forces just in case others are also doing so.

In a world where there is restraint at low numbers, the possibility of 'break-out' would still exist, with a nuclear-armed state covertly increasing its arsenal or a non-nuclear state developing a nuclear capability under the guise of a civilian programme. The perceived benefits that might be gained from such a break-out, however, would be far fewer than in a world where

---

[2] The author is grateful to James Acton for this point.

nuclear weapons had been 'abolished'. The risks of such a scenario could be reduced further, especially for states which see themselves as conventionally weak, by retaining some low-readiness 'second-echelon' nuclear hedge capabilities.

The ambition to achieve nuclear abolition will remain a powerful normative element in world politics. Mutual nuclear restraint would be an important step in the direction of reducing nuclear risks. Yet, with perhaps 2,000 weapons remaining in national arsenals, things could still go wrong, triggering a nuclear catastrophe comparable to, or even more damaging than, the major wars of the twentieth century.

The frequency and destructiveness of inter-state war has declined sharply over the last sixty years, and it is possible that this trend could continue and consolidate in the decades ahead. The conditions for a world war that would threaten the existence of any of the world's most economically powerful states, which in turn were the prime drivers for the original creation of nuclear weapons in the 1940s, no longer exist. None of the world's major powers is controlled by militarist or revolutionary ideologues, willing to risk everything for the sake of continental domination. The states of Western Europe – now joined by those of Eastern Europe – have stopped preparing for war with each other, as have most other high-income democracies.

More limited forms of conflict between the world's most powerful states are still plausible. Territorial disputes over maritime resources remain unresolved. Conflict could be triggered by the commitment of the US and its allies to humanitarian (and other) interventions, especially when these encroach on the interests of other major powers. Weak states (and non-state groups) continue to have an interest in precipitating external intervention in civil wars. Stronger states (such as Iraq in 1990 or Pakistan in 1999) could still miscalculate the response to acts of territorial aggression.

Few if any of these scenarios would bring nuclear weapons into play: the stakes would simply not be high enough. Yet, until war between Russia, India, China and the US becomes as unthinkable as it already is between OECD states, it is hard to imagine any of these major powers being prepared to give up a 'just-in-case' minimum nuclear force. Political relations between the US and Russia, or between the US and China, by contrast, might not have to get much better to create the conditions for mutual nuclear restraint at low numbers. Even if a more radical transformation in these relationships is not yet possible, such restraint could make a useful contribution to the wider process of peace-making between the major powers. The knowledge of what nuclear war is likely to mean is a permanent factor in human affairs. Whether, and in what form, this will require nuclear weapons to be maintained is a more open question.

About Whitehall Papers

The *Whitehall Paper* series provides in-depth studies of specific developments, issues or themes in the field of national and international defence and security. Published occasionally throughout the year, *Whitehall Papers* reflect the highest standards of original research and analysis, and are invaluable background material for specialists and policy-makers alike.

About RUSI

The Royal United Services Institute (RUSI) is an independent think tank engaged in cutting-edge defence and security research. A unique institution, founded in 1831 by the Duke of Wellington, RUSI embodies nearly two centuries of forward thinking, free discussion and careful reflection on defence and security matters.

RUSI consistently brings to the fore vital policy issues to both domestic and global audiences, enhancing its growing reputation as a 'thought-leader institute', winning the Prospect Magazine Think Tank of the Year Award 2008 and Foreign Policy Think Tank of the Year Award 2009 and 2011. RUSI is a British institution, but operates with an international perspective. Satellite offices in Doha and Washington, DC reinforce its global reach. It has amassed over the years an outstanding reputation for quality and objectivity. Its heritage and location at the heart of Whitehall, together with a range of contacts both inside and outside government, give RUSI a unique insight and authority.

For Product Safety Concerns and Information please contact our EU
representative GPSR@taylorandfrancis.com Taylor & Francis Verlag GmbH,
Kaufingerstraße 24, 80331 München, Germany

Printed and bound by CPI Group (UK) Ltd, Croydon, CR0 4YY
11/04/2025
01843992-0020